# THE INTELLIGENCE WAR

# THE INTELLIGENCE WAR

## DONALD P. STEURY

### Series Editor: Lieutenant Colonel Roger Cirillo, United States Army, Retired

MetroBooks

# MetroBooks

An Imprint of Friedman/Fairfax Publishers

©2000 by Michael Friedman Publishing Group, Inc.

Library of Congress Cataloging-in-Publication Data available upon request.
ISBN  1-56799-958-1

Editors: Ben Boyington, Sharyn Rosart
Art Director: Kevin Ullrich
Photography Editor: Chris Toliver
Production Manager: Camille Lee

Color separations by Bright Arts Graphics (S) Pte Ltd.
Printed in China by Leefung Asco Printers Ltd.

10 9 8 7 6 5 4 3 2 1

For bulk purchases and special sales, please contact:
Friedman/Fairfax Publishers
Attention: Sales Department
15 West 26th Street
New York, NY 10010
212/685-6610   FAX 212/685-1307

Visit our website:
http://www.metrobooks.com

# Contents

# The Secret War

## Lt. Col. Roger Cirillo (Ret.)

Professor Harry Hinsley, former Bletchley Park code breaker and official historian of British intelligence in World War II, noted that apart from more "open" sources—such as the press or government embassies in foreign lands—the British government received information on the enemy from four major covert sources, which he described as "physical contacts," including documents or prisoner interrogations; espionage; aerial photographic reconnaissance; and signals intelligence. None was a new source in World War II (and virtually every combatant nation relied upon the same four), but the extent to which those sources were exploited constituted a revolution in the art of intelligence. Moreover, the level of success each side enjoyed in gathering and interpreting intelligence was among the key elements upon which victory or defeat turned.

During the war, intelligence production in the Allied camp increased dramatically as the relatively low number of peacetime practitioners burgeoned to include thousands of analysts, code breakers, technical specialists, and even covert operators. These ranks were swelled not just with the Oxford dons, professors, lawyers, and ivy league gentlemen depicted in popular spy novels, but also with

a less glamorous host from every walk of life. Virtually every human skill was put to use in the intelligence network.

Once information was collected, processed, analyzed, and assessed, a central question arose: was the intelligence actually usable by those fighting the war, by those in charge of policy? The answer is as complicated as the history of the war itself. While more and better intelligence clearly enhanced the ability to estimate an enemy's capabilities, these capabilities were not always a reliable predictor of enemy intentions. Even when advances in code breaking pointed directly to an opponent's next move, the enemy was did not always act on its orders (as the Allies found out in North Africa during the winter of 1942–43). Nor was every move telegraphed by breakable codes, seen in advance by agents in the field, or observed by specialized reconnaissance aircraft.

Often, "hard" intelligence was denied to those who needed it most. Sometimes, decisions limiting the number of people who received intelligence were made to "protect the source," whose value was considered greater than the value of gaining a local tactical advantage. The secrecy required in

handling and distributing intelligence further complicated its use, as even those earmarked to receive intelligence were sometimes inadvertently denied it, or received it in such delayed or diminished form that it was unusable.

The most frequently heard complaint of intelligence specialists themselves was that high-level decision makers sometimes "ignored" key intelligence. These same specialists, however, rarely acknowledged that operations could not be changed instantly, that commanders often chose to risk the enemy's predictable reactions, and that sometimes battle was unavoidable, even under unfavorable circumstances. Risk is part of the commander's burden, and with timely and accurate intelligence, can be reduced. But not every commander found good intelligence available, particularly at the lowest levels, and hence the "intelligence man" was sometimes ignored. Moreover, perfect intelligence did not improve the military capability of poorly trained, under-supplied, or exhausted forces in the field. Merely knowing what the enemy might do, or where he was located, did not guarantee (though it usually improved the chances of) success.

Still, some policy makers and commanders could and did act against good advice, following their own preconceptions with disastrous results. Any study of the major intelligence failures of the war reveals a litany of bad decisions that, with the benefit of hindsight and without knowledge of the intangible influences on the decision makers that went unrecorded, are difficult to understand. Or perhaps it is just that the names and stories of the war's defeated commanders are well known while the names and stories of their intelligence officers are not.

Today, following a generation of Cold War during which intelligence was given high priority and nearly unlimited budgets, it is generally forgotten that the intelligence agencies of World War II were frequently offshoots of under-funded and understaffed departments, and that few professional intelligence analysts, operatives, and technologists existed when the war broke out. The United States in particular suffered heavily for the lack of a well-developed intelligence structure at war's start. The fact that its intelligence capabilities were developed quickly is due not only to the dedicated efforts of those assigned to the intelligence services, but by the infusion of help and information given by the other Allied governments.

A half century after the guns were stilled, information about the Secret War continues to be revealed. Long hidden from general view, it is a critical part of the history of World War II.

Roger Cirillo
Lt. Col., U.S. Army (Ret.)

Allied agents prepare for a drop into enemy territory. Specially trained "Jedburgh" teams were dropped into German-occupied France to help prepare the ground for the Normandy invasion. Though covert sabotage operations like this one had little to do with intelligence-gathering, they were managed by the same organizations that conducted intelligence operations.

# The Intelligence Century

Militarily speaking, the twentieth century could be called the intelligence century. Spies and spying are as old as history itself, but it is only in recent times that their function has been deemed important enough for intelligence to be formalized as a profession. This was due in part to the complexities in intelligence introduced by industrialization; in part to the enhanced destructiveness of modern weapons, which made it vital to track weapons developments as thoroughly as possible; and in part to the introduction of new intelligence technologies (such as aerial reconnaissance and signals intelligence), which required a greater level of professional skill.

Nevertheless, intelligence has remained a profoundly conservative profession, with traditional means of collection (which is to say, spying) predominating until well into this century. Much intelligence also was drawn from the reports of military attachés. This has meant that the most successful intelligence services were those that were able to draw upon the loyalties of very few people operating in what were often very dangerous circumstances. It was only during World War II that this began to change significantly. Thus, the intelligence history of the war is largely the story of the introduction of new

The memory of Feliks Dzerzhinsky, founder of the formidable Soviet secret police and intelligence establishment, is revered in Russian intelligence circles even today.

technologies of collection and new forms of exploitation of intelligence sources.

Without question, the most efficient intelligence service of this century was that of the Soviet Union. The Soviet leadership inherited a strong intelligence tradition from the Tsarist regime. Shortly after the October Revolution, the Soviets created their own

intelligence and security service, *Vserossiiskaya Chrezvychainaya Komissiya po Borbe s Kontrrevolyutsiei i Sabotazhem* (mercifully abbreviated to *Cheka*) under the leadership of Feliks Edmundovich Dzerzhinsky, a Pole born in Lithuania. "Iron Feliks" (an appellation applied first to the man and then to his statue outside KGB headquarters in Moscow) built the Cheka into a ruthless and effective service. In February 1922 the Cheka was incorporated into the Ministry for Internal Affairs (NKVD); in July 1923 it was renamed the OGPU (*Obyeddinenoye Gosudarstvennoye Politicheskoye Upravlenie*). In July 1934 it once again became known as the NKVD, and in February 1941 it became the NKGB (People's Commissariat for State Security); the term "KGB" was not introduced until the 1950s).

Through the period between the two world wars, the Soviet intelligence services were able to draw upon the loyalties of socialists and communists throughout the world. The Kremlin also was able to portray itself as the center of resistance to fascism in the 1930s—particularly when the Soviet regime and the Comintern (Communist International, the international organization of Communist parties run from and subordinate to Moscow) aided the Spanish loyalists in their fight against Franco and his fascist supporters in the Spanish Civil War. The NKVD and Soviet Military Intelligence (the GRU) were able to exploit these sympathies to build up a world-wide network of secret agents, or "moles," in influential places in the political and adminis-trative structures of all the great powers. The most famous ring of moles was the "Cambridge Comintern" (known in Soviet intelligence circles as "the Magnificent Five")—Anthony Blunt, Guy Burgess, Donald MacLean, Kim Philby, and John Cairncross—so-called because they were all recruited, along with an American, Michael Straight, while students at Cambridge University. A noteworthy GRU mole was the German jour-nalist Richard Sorge, who winnowed his way into the German embassy in Tokyo in the years before World War II. The NKVD also had a whole cluster of espionage rings throughout Western Europe, mostly operating independently of each other, that collectively have come to be known as the *Rote Kapelle*, or "Red Orchestra," the name given them by German intelligence.

Opposed to this formidable organization was a fairly thin line of Western intelligence services. At the end of World War I, the British all but completely dismantled their intelligence and signals intelligence organizations. Their foreign intelligence service, the SIS (Secret Intelligence Service, also known as MI-6) sur-vived only because its chief in 1919, Captain Sir Mansfield Cumming (also known, like all heads of SIS, as "C"), had secured control of the Passport Control Office, which was responsible for issuing visas in every British consulate and embassy in the world. PCO, or "Passport Control Officer" was the cover under which British intelligence officers oper-ated around the world. By the outbreak of war in 1939, however, PCO cover had worn

Sir Mansfield Cumming, known as "C", head of the British Secret Intelligence Service in 1919, preserved Britain's World War I intelligence capabilities under cover of the Passport Control Office (PCO), thereby establishing a comprehensive cover system that was to remain in force—albeit with diminished utility—until the outbreak of World War II.

so thin that it was little more than a not-very-convenient fiction. SIS officers survived only because, in accordance with SIS policy, they seldom collected intelligence against the country in which they were stationed, and frequently cooperated with the local service. British intelligence officers thus tended to be stationed in small, neutral countries located adjacent to one of the great powers.

In 1919, the British took a vitally impor-tant step when they preserved the bones of their formidable wartime signals intelligence organization in the Government Code and Cypher School (GC&CS), hidden away at Bletchley Park, an estate just outside London. At first under the Admiralty, in 1924 Bletchley

Park (the Royal Navy High Command) was transferred to the Foreign Office. Bletchley Park's task was to study foreign code and cipher systems around the world, especially those of possible British enemies. It was Bletchley Park that achieved the greatest intelligence success of World War II when its code-breakers penetrated the German ENIGMA codes. The head of the GC&CS from 1919 until 1942 was Commander Sir Alistair Denniston. In 1939, "C," the head of SIS, was Major-General Sir Stewart Menzies.

Under Adolf Hitler, the German intelli-gence establishment was subject to the same administrative chaos that prevailed generally in the Third Reich. In theory, the principal military intelligence organization was the *Abwehr*, headed by Admiral Wilhelm Canaris from 1935 on. The Abwehr ran most of the foreign intelligence operations. But the SS had its own intelligence service, the *Reichsicherheitshauptamt* (RSHA), under the sinister, murderous Reinhard Heydrich, who was also responsible for sending killing squads into the conquered Eastern territories to round up Jews, gypsies, and anyone else deemed racially inferior by Nazi doctrine. The German foreign office ran an intelligence service, and in the 1930s Hermann Göring, the chief of the *Luftwaffe* (the German air force), had his own organization for tapping embassy telephones and intercepting diplo-matic telegrams. This organization, called the *Forschungsamt*, was in addition to the regular Luftwaffe intelligence staff. The army and navy also had their own intelligence organizations, as well as signals intelligence collection units that, for the most part, were highly effective—although they all failed to detect Allied penetration of the ENIGMA machine cipher upon which virtually all German wireless communications depended. In the field, special signals intelligence units, or *Horchkompanien*, were an essential component of German military victories in the first part of the war. The navy's *Funk-Beobachtungsdienst*, or *B-dienst*, played a similarly vital role during the war, with detachments aboard all major warships, as well as at the main naval headquarters in Berlin and at U-boat High Command in Paris.

But all this success at tactical and operational levels could not compensate for generally inadequate strategic intelligence. Germany paid a heavy price for its racial chauvinism and retreat from world-trade markets in the 1930s. Its overseas presence by the outbreak of war was minimal and largely isolated. Its agents outside pro-Axis Europe were quickly rendered ineffective. British counterintelligence identified all German

Reinhard Heydrich, the vicious head of the Reichsicherheitshauptamt. To his left is the Reichsführer-SS, Heinrich Himmler. Together, these two established the SS as a "state within a state" in Nazi Germany.

agents in British and Commonwealth territories shortly after the outbreak of war. All were soon neutralized, and most were "doubled"— that is, they worked for British intelligence while still reporting to Berlin, thus becoming channels through which the British could feed false information to the enemy. In fact, the British soon found the existing sources available to the Germans to be inadequate and began inventing agents of their own to provide the kind of misinformation they wanted the Germans to have.

The Abwehr's record did not measure up to its reputation. Canaris became obsessed with bureaucratic infighting and with plotting against the evil regime he served. Beginning in 1942, most of the Abwehr's functions were stripped away by other organizations. Canaris himself increasingly suffered from bouts of depression. In 1944 he was implicated in the German generals' plot against Hitler, and in 1945 he was executed.

After the Soviet Union, fascist Italy probably had the most efficient intelligence service of the Great Powers. Italy's principal foreign intelligence arm was the *Servizio Informazioni Militari* (SIM), an army unit that usually was subordinate to the War Ministry, but during wartime to the Italian Supreme Command (*Commando Supremo*). As was so often the case in the early twentieth-century intelligence organizations, SIM's area of operations extended much farther than its purely military antecedents would suggest. Beginning in 1928, SIM supported Croatian and Macedonian terrorist groups in their efforts to overthrow the Serb-backed Royal Yugoslav government; in 1934, it helped the Croatian Ustashe assassinate King Alexander. SIM also backed Ethiopian dissident groups working against Emperor Haile Selassie and aided Palestinian groups in resistance against the British. When Italy invaded Ethiopia in

Pictured in Munich in October 1938, Adolf Hitler (second from right) and Benito Mussolini (far right) had formed an unofficial "Rome-Berlin axis" in 1936; it was formalized in 1939. Behind them are Mussolini's son-in-law and foreign minister, Count Galeazzo Ciano (second from left) and Germany's Field Marshal Hermann Goering (far left).

1935, SIM kept Mussolini abreast of British naval movements through signal decrypts and also sabotaged Ethiopian attempts to buy arms abroad. It also plotted to assassinate Haile Selassie, a move ultimately vetoed by Mussolini. Throughout the 1930s and beyond, SIM had spectacular success in stealing secret information from all of the foreign embassies in Rome.

The wartime head of SIM was Colonel Cesare Ame. One of Ame's first tasks was to rescue Italy's army in Greece, which was then floundering in the mountains on the Albanian border. In April 1941, as the German invasion from the north brought Yugoslavia into the war, Ame saved Italy's forces in Albania by intercepting and subverting the Yugoslav General Staff's orders to its units, keeping them immobile and confused. Nevertheless, SIM was much reduced in September 1941 when military intelligence sections were farmed off to the newly created army intelligence arm (*Servizio Informazioni dell'Esercito*). Much less well known was the Italian naval intelligence unit, *Servizio Informazioni Segreto* (SIS). The intelligence arm of the Italian air force was the *Servizio Informazioni dell'Aeronautica* (SIA).

In striking contrast to the effectiveness of Italian intelligence was the ineffectiveness of the Japanese intelligence services. In truth, the Japanese had built up a well-deserved reputation for intelligence operations in the prewar years, but they proved utterly incapable of meeting the demands of the Pacific War. In peacetime, Japanese agents in Hawaii were quite ingenious in locating individual U.S. warships and in passing diagrams of Pearl Harbor to naval planners in Tokyo, but they were rounded up on the outbreak of war. While Japanese signals intelligence organizations could achieve only minimal success against the Allies, Japanese wireless communications became more and more transparent as the war progressed. In particular, the Japanese proved to be even more dilatory than the Germans in detecting Allied penetration of their ENIGMA ciphers: one of the Allies' best sources was the Japanese ambassador to Berlin, General Oshima Hiroshi, who transmitted regular, detailed reports of the German war effort to Tokyo. Each message was intercepted and read by the Allies almost as quickly as it was received in Japan. The Japanese did prove much more effective in intelligence operations close to home—in China, in Burma, and in exploiting Indian nationalist sentiments against the British Raj—while their internal security was terrifying and brutally effective.

TOP: Admiral Wilhelm Canaris, chief of German military intelligence, had a sinister reputation but was only moderately effective as an intelligence chief. BOTTOM: Brigadier General William J. "Wild Bill" Donovan, a Wall Street lawyer, served as President Franklin D. Roosevelt's principal intelligence advisor and was chosen by him to head the Office of Strategic Services (OSS), the wartime U.S. intelligence agency. Donovan earned the nickname "Wild Bill" after winning the Medal of Honor in World War I.

The United States lacked an independent intelligence organization until after it entered World War II. Instead, the various government agencies divided up responsibilities for the collection of intelligence. There was no effort to coordinate activities or any formal mechanism to share information. Thus, foreign service officers collected political and economic intelligence for the Department of State in the course of their normal duties, while the army's Military Intelligence Division (MID) and the Office of Naval Intelligence (ONI) concentrated on their own areas of interest, mainly through attaché reporting. There was, in addition, Herbert O. Yardley's notorious "Black Chamber," funded by the Department of State, with the general responsibility for signals intelligence. The Black Chamber was quite effective in breaking diplomatic and military codes and ciphers and contributed significantly to the interwar naval arms control negotiations pushed by Washington and London.

But American isolationism and revulsion at the terrible losses of World War I kept funding for intelligence operations at a parsimonious level. In addition, all three government agencies wasted a good deal of time and energy combating an imagined threat of Red Revolution. Yardley's Black Chamber even targeted Canadian communists, through Comintern communiqués intercepted in a covert operation as far away as Riga, Latvia. In 1929 the incoming Secretary of State, Henry L. Stimson, abolished the Black Chamber on the excuse that "Gentlemen do not read other gentlemen's mail." Signals intelligence simply moved into the military agencies, however, especially into the army, where legendary cryptographer William F. Friedman had great success in breaking Japanese codes and ciphers, including their ENIGMA machine ciphers.

Nonetheless, the United States continued to suffer from an inability to coordinate the

Hitler greets the Japanese ambassador, General Oshima Hiroshi. Oshima regularly reported to Tokyo on the German war effort, using the Japanese diplomatic cipher. His reports were regularly read by Western intelligence agencies, which found them an invaluable source of information.

collection and dissemination of intelligence information, a flaw that was generally perceived to have contributed to the success of the surprise attack on Pearl Harbor in December 1941. Shortly thereafter, Roosevelt brought in Brigadier General William J. Donovan to organize the first U.S. intelligence agency, initially as Coordinator of Information, then as director of the Office of Strategic Services (OSS). Although the OSS usually is identified as the forerunner of the postwar Central Intelligence Agency (CIA), the OSS in fact operated exclusively under wartime conditions and had only a tenuous link to the postwar world.

It is safe to say that, in general, none of the intelligence services of the Great Powers were ready for the war in which they were to find themselves. Although the Western intelligence services certainly were more successful in the war than those of either the Soviet Union or the Axis powers, their effectiveness owes more to a greater flexibility once war broke out than to any prewar preparation or planning. Perhaps because they were the tools of democracies less bound by considerations of military caste, they were better able to adapt to changing circumstances. Certainly the wartime intelligence organizations of both Great Britain and the United States were noteworthy for the numbers of civilians and nonprofessional soldiers who achieved high rank and positions of great responsibility. And while it would be wrong to attribute the Allied victory wholly or even primarily to the Allies' superior ability to make effective use of intelligence in the long run, it also would be fair to say that there were a number of occasions when poor intelligence might have cost them the war. Certainly, without good intelligence, the Allied victory would have been longer in coming and would have cost many more lives.

# Chapter 1

# Blitzkrieg

THE RISE OF ADOLF HITLER AND THE THIRD REICH SET INTO MOTION THE events that led to the outbreak of World War II. Having assumed power in 1933, Hitler first broke down all opposition in Germany and then set about overturning the World War I peace settlement of Versailles and restoring German military power. In March 1938 he annexed Austria, and in September he bullied the Western powers into consenting to his occupation of the Sudetenland, the German-speaking Czech borderland. In March 1939 he engineered a coup in Slovakia as an excuse to occupy the remainder of the Czech state. The next month, he set his sights on Poland. Plans were laid for an invasion at the end of August 1939. This time, Hitler was set upon war.

Hoping to preserve the peace, Great Britain and France had given in to Hitler's demands in early 1938. In September, the British prime minister, Neville Chamberlain, and the French premier, Edouard Daladier, met with Hitler at Munich to negotiate a settlement over the Sudetenland. They yielded once again, but by the end of the year Chamberlain in particular had reluctantly concluded that war was inevitable. The following spring, he responded to the German occupation of Prague with a direct confrontation. On March 17, 1939, he publicly denounced the invasion. On March 31, Great Britain guaranteed Poland's territorial integrity; on April 13, following pressure from France, it extended a similar guarantee to Romania. To make good on these commitments, Great Britain did something that hitherto had been inconceivable: it sought a military pact with the Soviet Union.

The leader of the Soviet Union, Joseph Stalin, had been watching these events with no little interest and considerable irony. In 1938, he had tried to build a united front against Hitler, but had been rebuffed by the West. In any case, that same year

Despite the aura of invincibility that surrounded the German army at the onset of World War II, Germany was actually ill-prepared for a European war, lacking reserves or even long-term sources of supply. Tanks such as these Panzer IIs, lightly armed and armored, were overmatched by all but the most ineffective Allied tanks.

The British Secret Intelligence Service spread a thin network of listening posts, or "stations," across Europe in the years before World War II. Operating out of British legations, each station consisted of a very few officers whose job it was to collect intelligence on the other Great Powers. Built to monitor the Soviet Union, the British intelligence net began to focus on Nazi Germany late in 1938. The Stations, and their heads, were: Athens (Crawford), Belgrade (Maj. L.L. Buckland), Berlin (Maj. Frank E. Foley), Brussels (Col. Edward Calthrop), Bucharest (Edward G. Boxshall), Budapest (Capt. E.C. Kensington), Copenhagen (Bernard J. O'Leary), Helsinki (Harry L. Carr), Istanbul (Dick Lefontaine), Madrid (Hamilton-Stokes), Paris (Wilfred A. Dunderdale), Prague (Harold C.L. Gibson), Riga (Leslie Nicholson), Rome (McKenzie), Sofia (Teddy Smith-Ross), Stockholm (Lt. Cmdr. John Martin), Tallinn (Maj. Giffey), Vienna (Capt. Thomas Kendrick; from September, George Berry), and Warsaw (Col. J.P. Shelley).

## Britain's Man in Riga

Being a British intelligence officer was a lonely job: working on their own for the most part, officers of the Secret Intelligence Service (SIS) were placed in neutral capitals, under tissue-thin cover as "Passport Control Officers." They seldom collected intelligence on the country in which they were based, but ran networks of agents that operated inside the Great Powers.

Typical was Leslie Nicholson, Britain's "Man in Riga" from 1934 on. Described by a colleague as "very Black Watch, with the most incredibly polished shoes," Nicholson was unmarried, spoke fluent French and German, and had the advantage of an army pension to supplement his meager SIS salary. Recruited in 1931, Nicholson was hustled off to Prague, where he became involved in a lunatic scheme to build an atomic bomb in the basement of a Czech castle. In 1934, Nicholson was transferred to Riga, where he collected intelligence on the Soviet Union and, later, on Nazi Germany.

During his time in Riga, the capital of Latvia, Nicholson met a number of characters, including "Uncle Sebastian," a White Russian cavalry officer who ran a spy ring in the Soviet Union; Artur Schmidkoff, the head of Latvian internal security, who used a skull as an ashtray and described himself as "the most feared man in Latvia"; and a "very beautiful White Russian girl named Nina," who was almost certainly working for the Soviet Union, and probably for the Japanese as well.

In October 1938, Nicholson was joined by SIS veteran Kenneth Benton and his wife, Peggy, who wrote a memoir of their time in Riga, titled *Baltic Countdown*. With the outbreak of war, everyone, including Peggy, helped out in processing intelligence and obtaining visas for the streams of refugees pouring into Riga from all over Eastern Europe. In June 1940, the Red Army occupied Latvia, and Nicholson and the Bentons embarked on an epic train journey that took them across the Soviet Union to Vladivostok, and thence across the Pacific to the United States and, finally, home.

## SIS Stations in Europe in 1938

Stalin had reacted to a rumored coup in the Soviet military with a massive purge that decimated the Soviet officer corps and left the Red Army in no condition to fight a major war. Thus, in 1939 he resolved to strike a deal with Hitler that would allow him to stand back from the coming conflict. By the time he was approached by the British Foreign Office, he was already negotiating secretly with Hitler's foreign minister, Joachim von Ribbentrop, using the NKVD as an intermediary. Stalin then used negotiations with the British and the French as leverage to pressure Hitler into a deal.

Late in August 1939, with his troops massed on the Polish border, Hitler agreed. On August 22, Ribbentrop boarded a Lufthansa FW-200 and flew to Moscow. The next day, he negotiated a non-aggression pact with Stalin and his foreign minister, Vyacheslav M. Molotov. By secret codicil, Stalin agreed to allow Hitler to attack and destroy Poland in exchange for Soviet control of the eastern half of the country and a free hand in Finland, Latvia, Estonia, and Romanian Bessarabia (Moldova). (Hitler later exchanged Lithuania for more territory in Poland.) A week later, the German army attacked Poland. World War II had begun.

More than anything else, the willingness to appease Hitler that produced this dramatic string of German victories may be attributed to Allied failure to understand either Hitler or the Nazi regime. On one hand, neither the Western Allies nor the Soviet Union realized how far Hitler's ruthlessness or will to destroy would take him; on the other hand, they grossly overestimated the size and effectiveness of the German military. At least in part, these were basic intelligence failures.

In fact, it was all a gigantic bluff. Germany had a highly developed industrial sector, but lacked oil and essential raw materials. German rearmament would not even have been possible had France, Belgium, and Sweden not sold Hitler the iron ore and steel he needed to build up his war machine. As it was, in September 1939 the German military was only marginally better prepared for war than its enemies were. The German army lacked fuel, munitions, transport, and tanks: half the tanks that went into Poland and a third of those that were used to attack France were either captured from Czechoslovakia in March 1939 or built in Czech

ABOVE: A Czech woman is forced to welcome German troops occupying the Sudetenland in October 1938. Overawed by the specter of German military strength, the Western powers gave way when Hitler first annexed Austria in March 1938 and then demanded the Sudetenland. In doing so, Great Britain and France condemned the Czech population to a brutal Nazi occupation that lasted seven years. They also delivered intact to Hitler the Czech complex of military factories, one of the largest and most efficient in Europe, as well as a substantial steel industry and relatively large reserves of bullion. LEFT: German troops enter the Sudetenland. Although German doctrine emphasized the use of massed armored formations, German front-line forces included cavalry units until well into World War II.

TOP: Built according to a Czech design in Czech factories, Panzer 38t tanks like this one filled gaping holes in the German order of battle as Hitler deployed his armored striking forces against Poland. BOTTOM: Although Germany was not prepared for a long war in 1939, the effective use of tanks in massed formations gave the Third Reich the edge over countries like Poland, where cavalry charges were still part of the overall concept of war. Poland had tanks, too, but failed to use them as effectively as the Germans.

factories after the occupation. The *Luftwaffe* (the German airforce) lacked a usable long-range bomber, had no reserves of aircraft to replace losses, and suffered from a lack of munitions. The *Kriegsmarine* (the German navy) had been built up so rapidly that only a few of its major warships were ready for service. The German navy also suffered from a critical shortage of fuel oil, while its munitions shortages were even more severe than those of the army and air force.

The Western intelligence services had evidence of the economic problems the Germans faced, but responded with confusion and hesitation. Ironically, the French General Staff were reassured by reports from their air, military, and naval attachés in Berlin, who correctly reported that Germany was headed for war, but also correctly reported that the German war machine would not be ready for a long war until 1942. British intelligence puzzled over conflicting reports that showed, for example, airframe production in Germany at an all-time high but production of propellers, optics, and wheels for landing gears stagnant. Both kinds of information were true and reflected the inadequacies of the German war economy. Because aircraft could not fly without propellers, a failure to appreciate the meaning of all the reports taken together meant a tendency to overestimate the effectiveness of German military power.

The British Secret Intelligence Service was slow to respond to these developments and, in fact, remained focused on the Soviet Union until late in 1938. When Germany annexed Austria in March 1938, SIS officers in Vienna found themselves terribly exposed under their inadequate Passport Control Office cover. Ironically, when the Gestapo moved in, it left Captain Thomas Kendrick, the British intelligence chief, in place long enough to report on German saber-rattling for the move against Czechoslovakia that fall. On August 17, 1938, the Gestapo arrested Kendrick and subjected him to four days of brutal interrogation before sending him back to England. Immediately thereafter, the SIS withdrew Kendrick's staff from Vienna. SIS missions in Berlin and Prague soon were closed as well.

To compensate for the loss of reporting from Central Europe, SIS officer Kenneth Benton was sent to

# Frantisek Moravec

**Born in 1895, Frantisek Moravec was a student at the University of Prague (then in Austria-Hungary) when World War I broke out in 1914. One of his instructors was Thomas Masaryk, the future president of Czechoslovakia and founder of the independent Czech state. Being of military age, Moravec was quickly drafted into the Austrian army, where he found himself in command of a platoon of Czech troops. In January 1915, Moravec and his whole platoon defected to Russia, where they joined the independent Czech Legion.**

**At the end of the war, the Czech Legion fought its way across the span of the former Russian Empire, staying one step ahead of the Bolsheviks. When Czech Legionnaires returned to Prague, they provided much of the leadership for the new Czech military forces.**

**The chief of Czech military intelligence beginning in 1935, Moravec assembled an extensive network of agents working against Nazi Germany and the Soviet Union. After the Germans occupied Prague in March 1939, he essentially took these networks with him when he escaped to London, including the files on his agent in the Abwehr, Paul Thümmel, known to Czech and later British intelligence as A-54. Moravec was forced to leave his wife and two daughters behind in Prague, although he was able to engineer their escape before war broke out in September 1939.**

**From London, Moravec oversaw the activities of A-54 and worked on the London end of the Czech resistance movement. At war's end, he returned to Czechoslovakia, only to escape again in 1948, this time to Washington, D.C., to avoid the Soviets. Moravec took a job in the Pentagon and died of a heart attack in 1971.**

**Moravec's star agent, Paul Thümmel, remained active until March 1942, when he was arrested by the Gestapo. A high-ranking member of the Nazi Party, Thümmel was interrogated but otherwise left alone until just before the end of the war. His SS guards murdered him just before they evacuated his prison camp. Thümmel's motives for working for the Allies remain obscure. Although he was paid about $400,000 prior to 1939, he stopped accepting payment once Germany occupied Czechoslovakia. The information he provided was absolutely priceless.**

join PCO Leslie Nicholson in Riga, the capital of Latvia and a major listening post in northeastern Europe. The base at Riga was well-positioned to monitor German activity, but Nicholson—having spent the last six years building networks to operate against the Soviet Union—had few assets to report on the German target. Nicholson did put together the "Alex" network (so called because all the agents were code-named Alex: Alex 1, Alex 2, and so forth) in Germany, including one agent inside the giant Krupp armaments

combine, but his real strength was the relationship he had built up with the chief of Latvian military intelligence and with Artur Schmidkoff, the head of the Latvian Security Service.

Unfortunately for Nicholson, over the winter of 1938 to 1939, the Latvian government began to forge security ties with Germany in a vain effort to protect Latvia from Soviet aggression. On June 7, 1939, Latvia signed a non-aggression pact with Germany and about that time severed its relationship with British intelligence. Nonetheless, Nicholson continued to function, using the "Alexes," until the Soviet Union occupied Latvia in the summer of 1940. He also employed a cabaret singer named Ludmilla, who toured German ports on the

North Sea and Baltic coasts with her saxophone-playing husband and a copy of *Jane's Fighting Ships*.

Ironically, the SIS was most fortunate in Czechoslovakia, and scored an unexpected bonus out of the Munich crisis. The PCO in Prague was SIS veteran Harold C.L. Gibson. In Prague since 1934, Gibson had built up close relations with Czech military intelligence. The Czechs had a source inside the Luftwaffe General Staff: a man named Salm who reported on the buildup of the Luftwaffe until he was caught by the Gestapo and executed in 1937. Shortly after Salm was caught, the Czechs were approached by a senior Abwehr officer named Paul Thümmel. The first piece of information that Thümmel provided was the name of the Czech

German motorcycle troops, supported by an armored car, move into a Polish town bombed into rubble by the Luftwaffe. The non-motorized formations that comprised the majority of German infantry divisions often had trouble keeping up with the much faster mechanized units.

## Walter Schellenberg

Ruthless, ambitious, and cunning, German agent Walter Schellenberg was typical of the "new elite" who followed Hitler into power in 1933. In November 1939, Schellenberg, then head of the RSHA's Amt IVe, the SS counterintelligence service, organized a sting operation that lured two British SIS officers to Venlo, Holland. Schellenberg's most audacious (and ridiculous) operation was mounted the following year, when he traveled to Spain on Himmler's orders in an effort to kidnap the Duke and Duchess of Windsor, who were actually in Lisbon, Portugal, en route to the Bahamas.

In late 1941, Schellenberg took over Amt VI, the RSHA's foreign intelligence service, a post that put him into direct competition with Wilhelm Canaris, the head of the Abwehr (a bad place for Canaris to be). Schellenberg uncovered Canaris' role in the opposition to Hitler and personally arrested Canaris after the failure of the July 20, 1944, plot to kill Hitler. As a reward, Schellenberg was made head of the Abwehr.

The end of the war found Schellenberg in Sweden, attempting to negotiate peace terms through Count Folke Bernadotte, the vice president of the Swedish Red Cross and nephew of the king of Sweden. Bernadotte had agreed to act as mediator, subject to the release of Swedish and Norwegian political prisoners from the Sachsenhausen concentration camp. Following the German surrender in 1945, Schellenberg was extradited to stand trial at Nuremberg. He also served as a witness for the prosecution. Sentenced to six years in prison, Schellenberg was released in 1951. In 1952 he died of ill health in Switzerland.

Soviet premier Joseph Stalin was much better-served by his intelligence services than his contemporaries were, but he failed to exploit his advantage. Stalin's instinctive paranoia led him to mistrust his Western allies. Instead, the Soviet leader put his faith in the territorial guarantees offered by Hitler. Stalin tried to build a buffer zone between him and Hitler by annexing the Baltic states, eastern Poland, and part of Romania. He also hoped to buy off the Nazi leader with massive supplies of the raw materials German industry so desperately needed.

traitor who had fingered Salm. His own survival thus reasonably secure, Thümmel provided detailed information on the Abwehr, on the RSHA, and on the German armed forces' order of battle. In the summer of 1938, he brought advance warning of Hitler's plans to annex the Sudetenland.

The head of Czech military intelligence in 1938 was Major Frantisek Moravec. Despite the British and French betrayal of Czechoslovakia in September 1938, Moravec remained unshakably pro-British, and worked closely with Gibson, his SIS counterpart in Prague. When Thümmel brought details of Hitler's plans to occupy the rest of Czechoslovakia in March 1939, Gibson transported Moravec, his senior intelligence staff, and their files to Great Britain in advance of the German invasion. Thümmel remained in place, now reporting to London. He remained active until March 1942.

In intelligence, a very small number of people can make a tremendous difference. The intelligence provided by these very few agents and intelligence officers in Eastern and Central Europe had a decisive effect on British policy over the winter of 1938 to 1939. At least in part, the hardening of British attitudes that winter may be attributed to the increasingly dire war warnings that poured into Whitehall in December 1938 and January 1939 from SIS sources in Eastern Europe.

In Moscow, Stalin was well served by intelligence agents inside the German army, the Abwehr, and the British Foreign Office. He also regularly received intercepted British diplomatic cables. At bottom, however,

Stalin was deeply paranoid and trusted no one. He remained suspicious of British duplicity and did not trust the intelligence he received about British intentions, even though it came from highly reliable sources. Stalin's deal with Hitler was fairly typical, in that it relied on the seemingly concrete guarantee of a territorial buffer rather than on the less reliable guarantees made by foreign political leaders. Stalin also was obsessed about the possibility of internal dissent, which led him to accept false information about a plot inside the Soviet military that had been carefully leaked by German intelligence

The architects of the Nazi-Soviet non-aggression pact, Joachim von Ribbentrop (second from left) and Vyachislav Molotov (second from right), in Berlin in 1940.

the year before. The resultant "Great Purge" greatly frustrated much-needed efforts to modernize the army, so that the Soviet Union was not ready for war when it finally came. It was fairly typical of the intelligence situation in the Kremlin that the efforts of the most efficient service in Europe were frustrated by the prejudices and obsessions of the man at the top.

By August 1939, events in Eastern Europe were unfolding too quickly to be properly tracked from London. Ribbentrop's sudden trip to Moscow thus took Whitehall by surprise. When, on August 23, word came that Ribbentrop would make an important telephone call to Berlin that night, "C" instantly cabled Nicholson in Riga to find a way to tap into the telephone wires and listen in. Nicholson and his assistant, Kenneth Benton, spent a frantic eight hours trying to comply, only to discover that it was impossible: the telephone lines from Moscow to Berlin did not run through Latvia; they ran through Poland.

British intelligence had mistaken Riga for Warsaw. On this note of tragic farce, the Secret Intelligence Service entered World War II.

Within a week, Europe was at war. The German armies invading Poland from the west surrounded and destroyed much of the Polish army in the first two weeks of the war. The Soviet armies then moved into the eastern half of the country, and the destruction of Poland was complete. As the German army redeployed in preparation for the invasion of France, Moscow imposed "mutual security pacts" on the three Baltic states (Latvia, Estonia, and Lithuania) and forced them to accept Soviet garrisons. In November, the Soviet Union invaded Finland in an effort to secure the approaches to Leningrad. In this it was ultimately successful, but only after a war that lasted four months and cost the Soviets thousands of soldiers. The defense put up by the Finns made a mockery of Soviet military effectiveness and led foreign observers—especially the Nazi leadership—to conclude that the Soviet army was little more than a hollow shell. In June the Red Army occupied the Baltic states, and in October it moved into Bessarabia. Stalin's territorial defenses were complete.

In April 1940, Germany occupied Denmark and Norway in a shoestring amphibious operation that

The German military had a strong tradition of military intelligence. Shown here is Reinhard Gehlen (front row, center, with medal) and the staff of Fremde Heere Ost (FHO, or Foreign Armies East), the section of the General Staff responsible for collecting intelligence on the armies of Eastern Europe. Although usually associated with Operation Barbarossa, the German invasion of the Soviet Union, FHO was a long-established unit, and had concentrated initially on Poland.

ABOVE: Hermann Göring, the chief of the Luftwaffe, had his own private intelligence service, the Forschungsamt, which he used to intercept diplomatic telegrams and tap embassy phone lines in Berlin. Göring used the information provided by the Forschungsamt mainly in the internal struggles for power that characterized Hitler's Germany. RIGHT: London's docks burn after a 1940 German bomber raid. The Germans fatally overestimated their own strength and profoundly underestimated British resolve in the Battle of Britain. Even as bombs were falling on London, British cryptanalysts were achieving the intelligence breakthroughs that would help to turn the tide in World War II.

beat out by a matter of days an Allied Expeditionary Force on a similar mission. Barely a month later, the German army exploded across the border into France, Belgium, and Holland. Within six weeks, the German army had advanced all the way to the Channel coast and preparations were under way for the invasion of England. But Hitler was already planning the invasion of the Soviet Union the following year. When the Luftwaffe air assault on Great Britain failed to break the Royal Air Force that September, Hitler first postponed and then canceled the invasion. The defeat of Great Britain was left to the Kriegsmarine, which began an intensified assault on British supply lines in the North Atlantic.

In the intelligence war, as in the Allied war effort as a whole, the year following the fall of Poland was the blackest hour. British networks in Eastern Europe remained barely intact, largely because Hungary, Romania, and Bulgaria remained neutral for the time being, but the focus of the war was shifting westward and, for the moment, agents operating in the East had little to report. When, in the West, the SIS tried to make contact with what it believed was the German resistance, agents ran up against the RSHA's formidable counterintelligence chief, Walter Schellenberg. Taking a page from the Cheka's book, Schellenberg himself posed as a German officer opposing Hitler long enough to lure the SIS into a clandestine meeting at the Dutch border town of Venlo on November 9, 1939. In an audacious operation, Schellenberg captured two SIS officers and killed a Dutch intelligence officer. London was not even aware of what had happened until Reichsführer-SS Heinrich Himmler announced the results in a propaganda broadcast. After that, the British never trusted German resistance movements.

Meanwhile, in Riga, Leslie Nicholson continued to report on German naval activity, and attempted to supplement the Alex network with agents in German-occupied Poland, but he found his activities increasingly circumscribed by the growing Soviet presence in Latvia. When the Soviets invaded in June 1940, he left via the Trans-Siberian railway. His last reports described training exercises in the Baltic and the buildup of naval units in the North Sea and Baltic ports over the winter and early spring of 1940.

London failed to see the significance of this activity, however, so the German invasion and occupation of Norway and Denmark in April 1940 came as a complete surprise. By contrast, the invasion of France barely a month later was not unexpected, although the rapidity with which the Germans defeated the French army was a shock. Only the English Channel now stood between the German army and the conquest of the United Kingdom.

Even so, the seeds of victory were already being sown. In January 1940, British cryptographers had broken the first German codes. By the time the Luftwaffe began bombing Britain in September 1940, British intelligence was able to read enough traffic to predict when and where attacks would occur. British intelligence also monitored German preparations for invasion in the French and Belgian Channel ports.

On September 21, 1940, Britain's agent in the Abwehr, Paul Thümmel, reported that the invasion had been postponed. By the end of October, it was obvious from signals intelligence that the Germans would not invade Great Britain that year.

The key to all this was a little machine in a wooden box about the size of a typewriter: the ENIGMA machine.

# Chapter 2

# The Greatest Secret

In 1919, a Dutch inventor named Koch patented a design for an automatic cipher machine that relied on a series of rotors and variable electrical connections to encipher messages. In 1923 the rights to his design were purchased by a Berliner named Artur Scherbius, who sold his version of the machine to commercial firms in Germany and abroad. In 1929, however, Scherbius achieved what most inventors only dream of: he was bought out by the government. After examining Scherbius' device, the German defense ministry had seized upon it as a means of producing wireless communications that could not be read by an enemy signals intelligence unit. The Germans maintained this belief until the end of World War II. They were wrong. In a decade-long effort by Polish, French, and finally British cryptographers, the Allies had learned to break into the ciphers produced by the ENIGMA machine (as it came to be known) even before war began in 1939. Although very few messages could be read at first, the penetration of the ENIGMA ciphers broadened throughout the war until whole sectors of the German communications network were virtually transparent to Allied intelligence.

ENIGMA machine ciphers were extarordinarily difficult to break. In essence, the machine was a device for converting plain text or coded signals into a seemingly random series of letters; however, instead of being random, they actually followed predetermined settings. In theory, it was impossible to read the message unless you had an ENIGMA machine and knew what the necessary settings were. If you lacked either of these prerequisites, you were presented with a problem that had hundreds of millions of possible solutions, only one of which was correct.

Cracking the ENIGMA cipher meant, in effect, working through these hundreds of millions of solutions quickly enough for the intelligence derived from it to be of operational value. In practical terms, the

At Bletchley Park, the unlikely-looking home of the British Government Code and Cypher School, British cryptanalysts penetrated the German ENIGMA cipher.

Allied solution of the ENIGMA ciphers depended on three factors: an understanding of how the machine worked; a means of quickly working through a large number of possible solutions; and a number of procedural errors routinely committed by German wireless operators and other windfalls that significantly reduced the number of possible combinations that had to be tried.

When the German army and navy introduced their ENIGMA ciphers in the late 1920s, they proved to be insoluble. In 1932, however, Captain Gustave Bertrand of French military intelligence received pages of an ENIGMA instruction manual from an informant inside the German Ministry of Defense. Remarkably, neither British nor French intelligence expressed any interest in it: examining the information, they concluded that such a machine cipher would indeed be unbreakable and was therefore not worth pursuing. However, in December 1932, Bertrand visited the Polish Cipher Bureau in Warsaw and presented its commander, Major Gwido Langer, with his intelligence on the new German system.

Langer and Polish intelligence had already confronted the German ENIGMA, and had found it unbreakable by normal means. Armed with this new intelligence, however, a brilliant young Polish cryptographer named Marian Rejewski took up the challenge. Over the next few years, Polish intelligence was able to break into the ENIGMA codes and read a great deal of German wireless traffic, deciphering the signals laboriously, by hand calculations. By 1939 they had managed to reconstruct an ENIGMA machine to German specifications. In July, the Poles presented the British and the French with an example of their copy of the ENIGMA machine, along with the results of their research.

Unfortunately, after the war broke out, the Germans instituted changes in procedures and some alterations to their ENIGMA machines that countered the Polish breakthroughs. The Poles probably would have countered these obstacles in time, but they were overrun before they could do so. It is a tragic irony that, having contributed so much to the Allied victory, Poland ultimately benefited little from the heroic efforts of its signals intelligence experts.

In fact, the British Government Code and Cypher School at Bletchley Park had by this time started

OPPOSITE: Germany developed the ENIGMA machine as a means of guaranteeing the security of their communications in the field. Just a bit larger than a typewriter, the ENIGMA machine was easily transportable and could be used almost anywhere. Here, the staff of Panzer commander Heinz Guderian (standing) prepares to encipher a message on their ENIGMA. LEFT: To help decipher German ENIGMA communications, British cryptanalysts developed the "bombe," an analog computer capable of rapidly running thousands of possible combinations. Even so, it was difficult to keep up with the changes in the German codes and the volume of message traffic that was intercepted.

concentrating on breaking the ENIGMA codes, their work in some respects surpassing Polish efforts. By dint of hard work, genius, and sheer good luck, Bletchley Park circumvented the changes introduced by the Germans at the outbreak of war. But perhaps the most significant contribution initially made by Bletchley Park was the development of the "bombe," an early analog computer that duplicated the functions of an ENIGMA machine and made it possible to try out thousands of possible combinations at relatively high speed.

Even so, it often took time to break a cipher, especially since the Germans changed their machine settings daily. Bletchley Park was aided in its efforts by procedural errors committed by German operators and by clues sometimes provided by the duplication of signals,

or by guessing a signal's content through knowing the circumstances under which it was made. Luftwaffe signals were especially helpful in this regard. Luftwaffe radio security was terrible, and Luftwaffe pilots sometimes repeated by voice radio, in the clear, what was transmitted by wireless in cipher. In addition, the Luftwaffe maintained liaison officers, called "Flivos" (*Fliegerverbindungsoffiziere*), at German army headquarters. Their role was to coordinate army-Luftwaffe cooperation in ground operations, and they transmitted frequent signals in a code that was broken very early in the war. Because Luftwaffe operations often paralleled those of the army or the Kriegsmarine, their signals were often used to penetrate other forms of German military communications.

In a yearlong effort that was so intense it resulted in mental collapse, legendary American cryptanalyst William F. Friedman broke the Japanese diplomatic codes. Here, Friedman explains the principles of a cipher machine to Louise Newkirk, a new employee in the U.S. Army's Military Intelligence Division, in 1930.

Most important, however, was the capture of ENIGMA code books, manuals, and machines. Despite stringent German security, these captures occurred with remarkable regularity throughout the war. ENIGMA machines were secretly the targets of a number of British commando raids, for example. Whenever possible, British naval officers were directed to board German U-boats and retrieve ENIGMA machines and all the documentation they could lay their hands on. On May 9, 1941, a party from the destroyer HMS *Bulldog* boarded the scuttled German submarine U-110 as it was sinking and made off with a complete ENIGMA machine and several months' worth of settings and codebooks. Needless to say, the capture of such material was always kept highly secret, lest the Germans find out and change their settings or procedures.

Signals intelligence derived from reading German ENIGMA material was known as ULTRA. ENIGMA ciphers were used by the German army, the Kriegsmarine, the Luftwaffe, the SS, the German Foreign Office (*Auswärtiges Amt*) and the *Deutsche Reichsbahn Gesellschaft*, the state railways. Altogether, almost 200 separate ENIGMA ciphers were identified by the end of the war, though not all of them were broken. In 1941, still convinced that ENIGMA made their communications secure, the Germans forced their Italian allies to adopt a version of ENIGMA as well; as a result, Italian communications (hitherto largely unbroken) became readable by Allied cryptographers.

The Japanese also used a version of the ENIGMA machine, albeit one of rather different design. Japanese signals were especially difficult to read because of the complexity of the language, especially as written on cipher machines; even Japanese operators had to be specially trained. It was all the more difficult for Allied cryptographers, whose command of the language in any form was generally less than perfect.

Under the leadership of its chief cryptanalyst, William F. Friedman, the U.S. Army Signal Intelligence Agency broke the first Japanese code in 1940. The code, used in diplomatic communications, was known as MAGIC. The Japanese code machine that produced the messages was called PURPLE. Reading MAGIC, the army was able to monitor Japanese diplomatic communications between Tokyo and Washington, but failed to receive early warning of the attack on Pearl Harbor. The MAGIC secret was very closely held in any case, which may have contributed to the 1941 debacle at Pearl Harbor. By the spring of 1941, however, the United States was sharing MAGIC with Bletchley Park; in June a PURPLE machine was sent out to Singapore. Perhaps the most effective use of magic was in reading communications of Hiroshi Oshima, the Japanese ambassador to Berlin. Oshima provided Tokyo with regular, detailed reports on the German war effort that were of immense value to Allied intelligence analysts until the very end of the war.

During the war, Japanese military communications were classified under the ULTRA rubric, along with German communications. The United States had broken some Japanese naval ciphers before Pearl, but the real breakthroughs came later—in time to aid in the defeat of the Japanese Navy at the Battle of Midway.

What made both MAGIC and ULTRA so valuable was that the Germans and the Japanese (and even the Italians) were absolutely convinced that the use of ENIGMA cipher machines made their communications invulnerable. The intelligence derived from reading those signals, therefore, was completely reliable. Needless to say, the security surrounding ULTRA and MAGIC was very tight at all times. There were close calls, nonetheless, and security officers constantly feared that the secret might be revealed: the British knew, for example, that the French and Polish cryptographers captured by the Germans knew the ULTRA secret, but despite interrogation by the Gestapo, no one talked. The Japanese came close to capturing the PURPLE machine in Singapore. Most notoriously, the anti-Roosevelt *Chicago Tribune* ran a story after the Battle

of Midway that revealed the role played by signals intelligence—but somehow Japanese intelligence missed the story. Throughout the war, there was always the chance that the use of ULTRA in a military operation would reveal the secret to the enemy; in fact, evidence has recently been found to suggest that, in 1943, the German Flag Officer, Admiral Karl Dönitz, suspected that his communications were being intercepted and read and ordered an investigation. But the secret was kept.

Contributing to the effectiveness of the ENIGMA machine was its versatility. About the size of a typewriter, the ENIGMA machine could be used as easily in the field as at a military headquarters or on board a warship.

# Chapter 3

# Agents and Double Agents

ACCORDING TO ONE ESTIMATE, 80 PERCENT OF IMPORTANT INTELLIGENCE EVENTS
in World War II had to do with signals intelligence. It is hard to know how such a measurement was
derived, but it probably does accurately reflect the important role played by signals intelligence during the war. Always in the background, however, there was a secret war waged by men and women
who were frequently in very great danger and often engaged in seemingly very mundane tasks.

## The Rote Kappelle

The Soviet campaign to create networks of agents placed in positions
of importance throughout the world was remarkably successful. By the
time World War II broke out, Soviet intelligence agents had penetrated
to the highest levels of government in all the Great Powers. The most
important of these networks was the *Rote Kapelle* (as it was called
by German counterintelligence), or "Red Orchestra," that operated
throughout Europe. Actually, this was a complex of independent
networks run by the GRU (Soviet military intelligence), the most
important of which were in Germany, France and Belgium, and
Switzerland. All these networks had the same mission: to report on

Throughout Europe, men and
women risked their lives to
fight against the Nazi occupation. The risks of capture,
torture, and death were very
great, and meaningful results
often came only at great cost.
These men and women kept
hope of eventual victory alive
for millions of people living
under Nazi tyranny. Here,
French resistance fighters plan
an operation, probably part of
a training exercise in England.

Keep mum she's not so dumb!

CARELESS TALK COSTS LIVES

Britain, but also because, under Belgian law, espionage against other governments was perfectly legal. The head of the Belgian network was a veteran Soviet GRU (military intelligence) officer, Leopold Trepper. An experienced (and ruthless) professional, Trepper used at least twenty identities and had documents to prove his citizenship in five different countries. From 1936 to 1938, he was based in Paris but traveled widely throughout Western Europe and Scandinavia, setting up intelligence networks. Late in 1938, Trepper moved to Brussels, where he hooked up with an old friend and former Comintern agent, Leon Grossvogel. Trepper and Grossvogel started a legitimate business in Brussels, the Foreign Excellent Trench Coat Company, as a cover. Grossvogel now did most of the traveling for Trepper, but "Le Grand Chef," as he was called, remained in tight control. When the Germans overran France and the low countries, Trepper moved to unoccupied France but kept up his contacts in Paris and Brussels.

One strength of the Belgian network was that most of the staff of the Foreign Excellent Trench Coat Company actually knew nothing of the espionage for which it served as a cover. The legitimate activities of the firm helped to confuse the Gestapo for a while, but in August 1941, Walter Schellenberg's unit began to gradually draw all of Trepper's agents in by tracking down their wireless transmissions. Trepper himself was finally caught in December 1942, while visiting his dentist. Le Grand Chef coolly fed his interrogators the names of his least important agents and helped them trap more through false wireless messages, all the while protecting the core of the important agents in his network. In September 1943 he escaped, remaining at large until the end of the war, when, ironically, he was imprisoned by Stalin.

In Germany itself, Trepper's espionage network maintained contacts with three groups headed by Harro von Schulze-Boysen, Arvid Harnack, and Rudolf von Scheliha. Schulze-Boysen worked for counterintelligence in the German Air Ministry for a while, even though he was a known communist. In August 1942, he was arrested while encoding a message to Trepper giving the Luftwaffe order of battle deployed against the Soviet Union.

German actions and intentions. In this they achieved all that could be expected of them, but, as will be seen, much of their most important reporting was ignored or distrusted in Moscow.

The earliest networks were set up in Belgium because of its proximity to Germany, France, and Great

OPPOSITE: Allied counter-intelligence was constantly on the lookout for spies. The image of the spy as a glamorous seductress—as depicted in this British security poster—was more a way to focus attention on the threat of enemy agents than it was a reflection of reality. In fact, German spies were staggeringly ineffective in Allied countries, especially in Great Britain, where almost all the German agents were caught and "doubled." And none of them were women.

LEFT: Allied agents in German-controlled territory faced the brutal and formidable Nazi security apparatus, which was led by such luminaries as SS General Karl Alberecht Oberg, head of the Gestapo in occupied Paris. Oberg also helped to organize the deportation of forced labor into Germany and the implementation of the Final Solution in France.

RIGHT: German Pzkw 38t tanks of the Seventh Panzer Division advance into the Soviet Union. Soviet intelligence repeatedly warned the Kremlin of the impending German attack, only to be ignored by Stalin. As a result, the Germans achieved near-total surprise in the opening phases of the attack. The advancing German forces encircled and destroyed whole Soviet armies and ruthlessly destroyed everything in their paths, as the billowing black smoke in this photograph attests. But this time, the Wehrmacht was overmatched. The Soviet Union had spent the first two years of the war building itself up and modernizing its military equipment. The new Soviet tanks just coming into service, such as the famous T-34, were superior to the armored vehicles in the German Panzer divisions, many of which— including these Czech-built tanks—were already obsolete. OPPOSITE BOTTOM: Superior German training and tactics allowed them to compensate for the growing inferiority of their equipment, until new, better German tanks, such as the late-model Pzkw VI Tiger I, could be and deployed.

Arvid Harnack, another known communist, was a graduate of the University of Wisconsin, where he had earned a doctorate in economics. Harnack acted as liaison for a number of agents, including Schulze-Boysen, and was responsible for transmitting their material to Moscow, initially through his contacts in the Soviet embassy and then, after Germany invaded the Soviet Union, by wireless. He was caught and executed by the Germans in December 1942.

Rudolf von Scheliha was an especially valuable agent because of his important position in the *Auswärtiges Amt*, the German Foreign Office. A Soviet agent since 1934, Scheliha's last foreign post had been at the German embassy in Warsaw. Thereafter he was stationed in Berlin. Scheliha was not a communist; he sold the Soviets intelligence at rates running from $3,000 to $6,500 per report. Scheliha operated separately from the other agents, in part because he did not blend with the ideologically motivated Rote Kapelle networks, and in part because of his sensitive position inside the Auswärtiges Amt. The Gestapo nonetheless tracked him down in October 1942 during their campaign against the Rote Kapelle. He was executed in December 1942.

Each of these agents was at the center of his own network of informants and other agents and was, in turn, supported by GRU agents parachuted into Germany by the Red Air Force or brought in through Switzerland or some other neutral country. Altogether, the Rote Kapelle in Germany is estimated to have cost the German military about 200,000 lives, according to Abwehr chief Wilhelm Canaris.

The last important element of the Rote Kapelle was the so-called *Rote Drei*, or "Red Three," run by the Hungarian communist Sándor Radó in Switzerland. Radó ran several rings of agents, each of which were given female names. The most important was "Lucy," who penetrated into the very heart of the Abwehr. Lucy was Rudolf Rössler, a German communist who owned a map-publishing house in Lucerne, Switzerland. Rössler's business allowed him to travel extensively in

Germany, where he had three major sources: Hans Gisevius, a German diplomat and Abwehr agent who was stationed in Switzerland; Carl Goerdeler, the former mayor of Leipzig and a leader in the German resistance; and Generalmajor Hans Oster, who was the deputy chief of the Abwehr. All these sources (especially Oster) brought in high-level intelligence of considerable value concerning German intentions and strategic planning, but little was made of it in Moscow (see "Operation Barbarossa," below). Rössler was caught and imprisoned by the Swiss authorities in June 1944, but was later released. After the war, he was caught and again imprisoned, this time for spying for the communist Czech government. Goerdeler and Oster were implicated in the July 20, 1944, attempt on Hitler's life and executed. Gisevius worked for the OSS in Switzerland and survived the war.

ABOVE: Richard Sorge was the Soviet Union's agent inside the German embassy in Tokyo. A German Communist, Sorge began working for Soviet military intelligence (GRU) in the 1930s. Working under cover as a journalist, Sorge won the confidence of the German ambassador to Japan, Generalmajor Eugen Ott—even as he seduced his wife. Sorge, one of the Soviet Union's most valuable agents, provided accurate and timely warnings of the German attack on the Soviet Union. But Stalin despised and distrusted Sorge and ignored everything he reported. In 1941, Sorge was caught by the Japanese secret police and held for three years before being executed. In the 1960s, he was posthumously made a Hero of the Soviet Union.

# Operation Barbarossa

On June 22, 1941, Nazi Germany invaded the Soviet Union. In its opening stages, at least, Operation Barbarossa was a walk-over for the experienced troops of the German Wehrmacht. The Soviet Union was not prepared for war. Inexplicably, Soviet troops were deployed forward, just inside the border separating Soviet territory from Nazi-occupied Europe. As German armored forces drove deep into the captive Baltic states, Belarus, and Ukraine, the great fingers of the opening German offensive gathered these hapless Soviet ground forces into enormous encirclements to be slaughtered en masse or captured and driven into vast prisoner-of-war pens. Deployed west of the Daugava (Dvina) River, the vast bulk of the Red Air Force was caught on the ground and devastated by the lightning attacks of the Luftwaffe. Those Soviet fighters managed to stagger into the air proved to be no match for the experienced German pilots, who shot them down in droves. Fleeing from its recently acquired forward bases in Riga and Tallinn, the Red Banner Baltic Fleet was driven back into the Gulf of Finland by advancing German ground forces. Its battleships, cowering in Leningrad, did not even manage to put to sea before they were put out of action by German dive bombers. Meanwhile, the giant German battleship *Tirpitz* and the ships of the *Baltenflotte* arrogantly cruised off the mouth of the Gulf, awaiting any Soviet ships that should try to escape their fate by fleeing to Sweden. Everywhere, surprise was absolute: even as the Wehrmacht crossed the Soviet frontier, trains loaded with oil and grain were heading westward from Ukraine and the Caucasus into German-occupied territory.

This strategic surprise is even more remarkable considering how thoroughly Soviet intelligence monitored German intentions. This was, indeed, the moment for which Soviet intelligence agents had been waiting for more than a decade. In their supreme moment of trial, they did not let the socialist Motherland down. In fact, Joseph Stalin is known to have received at least eighty-four separate intelligence warnings of the impending German attack. The Rote Kapelle, in particular, reported correctly on German intentions throughout 1940 and 1941, and with increasing accuracy. The Kremlin also received warnings from the NKGB (successor to the NKVD and predecessor of the KGB) agents inside Whitehall and elsewhere, as well as from Richard Sorge in the German embassy in Tokyo. Most incredibly of all, at a luncheon early in June 1941, the German ambassador to Moscow—Friedrich Werner, Graf von der Schulenburg—took Stalin aside and told him:

> It is possible that nothing like this has happened in the history of diplomacy, but I am going to reveal to you our state secret number one…. Hitler has taken the decision to begin war with the Soviet Union on June 22. You will ask me why I am doing this. I was raised in the spirit of Bismarck, who was always an opponent of war with Russia.

All of this fell on deaf ears. Believing that Hitler would not attack the Soviet Union as long as Germany was still fighting Great Britain, Stalin regarded all warnings of an imminent German attack as false information planted by aristocrats in the German military or, worse, the British Secret Intelligence Service. When, on April 17, 1941, the GRU resident in Prague passed a warning that the Germans would invade in the second half of June, the Soviet leader scrawled across it in red ink: "English provocation. Investigate! Stalin."

In the early war years, the German army seemed invincible, as this dramatic photograph of advancing soldiers might suggest.

# The Resistance

To varying degrees, the Axis conquests in Europe (and, later, in Asia) produced active resistance movements in virtually every defeated country. In some cases, resistance began immediately, although at first the apparent hopelessness of the Allied military situation made it difficult to find people willing to risk their lives fighting the Nazis, especially after the fall of France. As the war dragged on, however, the strains of the Axis occupations—which, along with the hardships of rationing and shortages, also brought forced appropriations and conscripted labor—steeled public opinion against the occupiers and made it easier to recruit active resisters. Meanwhile, the gradual improvement in the Allied military position made it increasingly clear that the Axis occupation would not last forever. Ironically, the turning point in the European resistance came with the German invasion of the Soviet Union on June 22, 1941. This event brought the Communist parties in the occupied countries—hitherto quiescent because of the Molotov-Ribbentrop Pact—into the war against the

Axis. Schooled by generations of covert opposition to their own governments, the communist underground in several countries proved to be valuable assets in the war against the Axis.

To the extent that there was a unifying element in the resistance movements, it was provided by the British Special Operations Executive (SOE), later operating alongside the Special Operations Branch (SO) of the American OSS. The SOE dropped agents to work with the underground movements and provided arms, radios, and even training for resisters (most of whom had been civilians before the war, and had few military skills and little pertinent experience). In Scandinavia, the SOE even operated a regular transport service, the "Shetland Bus," between Scotland and Norway. From 1940 until late in 1944, Norwegian fishing boats plied back and forth, delivering agents and supplies and picking up refugees and others who needed transport to Britain. By the end of the war they had carried nearly 650 passengers and more than 300 tons (272,400kg) of weapons and supplies in just over 200 voyages.

Brutal German occupation policies won only the hatred of the peoples subject to their control and resulted in the rise of resistance movements that plagued the occupying forces. Here, German troops execute Polish prisoners in retaliation for the killing of a German soldier.

Equipped and supplied by the British Special Operations Executive (SOE), French resistance fighters harassed German occupying forces and launched raids against German lines of communication. But the risks were great and losses were heavy. Here, French *maquis* recruits learn to use a British-supplied Sten gun.

But there really was no single unified resistance movement; rather, the resistance operated in isolated groups, each with its own organization and goals. The communists in France, for example, had a very different view of the postwar world than their Gaullist counterparts. In Yugoslavia, Draža Mihailovich's royalist Chetnik partisans clashed as often with Tito's communists as they did with the German and Italian occupiers.

In addition, few groups knew anything about the activities of the others. This secrecy was necessary for security reasons: what the resisters did not know, they could not reveal under torture if they were caught. Most needed to work day jobs to live (as well as for cover purposes) and found themselves fighting instead of sleeping. Women proved especially useful in these actions, finding in covert warfare the combat roles that had been denied them in the regular militaries. Women also were freer to move about during the day: the occupying troops assumed as a matter of course that women seen on the streets during the day were engaged in some domestic errand, whereas men were supposed to be at their jobs.

Everyone involved in the resistance movement was in constant danger. Anyone could be wounded or killed during an operation; capture meant interrogation, torture, and almost certain death. And tragically, success in some operations—such as blowing up a train—often meant that innocent people would be killed in reprisals.

The resistance took as many forms as there were occupied countries. In France, organized groups—called *maquis*, after the brush covering the hills in which they hid—took advantage of the rough terrain in the southern part of the country to establish secret camps from which they mounted raids on the German garrisons. The communists concentrated on the cities and working class districts and even helped in the liberation of Paris. The human cost of resistance in France was high: more than 90,000 casualties among the freedom fighters by the end of the war, plus thousands more innocent people killed in reprisals.

In Norway, the underground army totaled more than 30,000, a remarkable figure in a country with a population of not much more than 2 million. By war's end, nearly 200,000 Norwegians had been imprisoned by the Germans for subversive activity. In Denmark and the Netherlands—small countries with few places to hide—

## Operation Freshman

For those few individuals who knew about the American atomic bomb program, the greatest fear was that the Germans would get the bomb first. It was known that Nobel laureate Werner Heisenberg, one of the fathers of quantum mechanics, was working on the atomic bomb for the Nazis. It was also believed that Heisenberg was building a reactor using heavy water as a moderator (the Americans used graphite). A crash program was launched to prevent Heisenberg from building that reactor.

As it happened, the only producer of heavy water on a scale sufficient to supply Heisenberg was the Norsk Hydro Plant at Rjukan, Norway. In November 1942, thirty-four British engineer troops were glider-dropped into Norway to destroy Norsk Hydro. This was the first British attempt to use gliders operationally, and it was a fiasco. All the aircraft crashed. Fourteen of the engineers were killed outright; the remaining twenty were captured by the Gestapo and executed.

In February 1943, the Allies tried again, this time with six Norwegian SOE agents under the command of Lieutenant Joachim Rönneberg. Although they landed far from their drop zone, Rönneberg and his men managed to find and damage Norsk Hydro enough to put it out of commission. On November 16, 1943, the plant was bombed by the U.S. Eighth Air Force, guaranteeing that it would never be restored to operation.

The Germans then tried to transport the plant's equipment and some heavy water out of Norway to Germany, where it would be safe from saboteurs, if not from Eighth Air Force bombers. This time, a Norwegian SOE team under the leadership of Knut Haukelid destroyed a ferry carrying the materials across Lake Tinnsjoie.

In fact, Heisenberg and his team probably were further away from perfecting a working bomb than anyone realized at the time. But the lack of heavy water was seen as a critical factor in delaying the German bomb. The destruction of Norsk Hydro was believed to have set back the German atomic bomb program by at least a year.

These Norwegian resistance fighters, captured by the Germans in December 1941, were lucky in that their death sentences were commuted. Luck is relative, however. Any captured resisters who weren't killed outright were forced to spend the rest of the war in a German concentration camp.

# Jacques Stosskopf

After the fall of France, the French navy came to an agreement with the Kriegsmarine by which the French would continue to operate the major naval facilities on the Bay of Biscay and in the English Channel for the benefit of the German naval units based there. In return, the French would be allowed to retain those bases during the period of the armistice. French naval personnel thus maintained the ship repair and docking facilities and worked on German warships. They were, in fact, vital to German conduct of U-boat and heavy-ship operations in the Atlantic. The chief French dockyard officer at the important U-boat base at Lorient was a naval engineer officer, Jacques Stosskopf, an Alsatian who spoke perfect German.

Although the Kriegsmarine took full advantage of the French facilities and made extensive use of the skilled French dockyard personnel, the Germans assumed that the naval facilities in occupied France were shot through with spies as a matter of course, and they were right. Every French naval base used by the Germans had a contingent of designated personnel who reported regularly to French naval intelligence, and through them to Allied intelligence organizations, usually American military or naval intelligence.

But the Germans did not suspect Jacques Stosskopf, who got on well with his fellow naval officers and apparently performed his job with enthusiastic efficiency. Stosskopf was given unlimited access to the German warships and was privy to the most sensitive information concerning their deployment and operation.

Actually, Stosskopf had been placed in Lorient on the orders of the chief of the Northern Section of the French intelligence service, a man named Trautman. Stosskopf went to Vichy at two- to three-month intervals, where, in the course of official business, he met with Trautman and provided him with memoranda or oral reports on the activities of the German U-boats based at Lorient. Trautman, in turn, passed these reports on to the American embassy. This was a very secure setup, but it lasted only as long as neutral Vichy remained unoccupied by German troops.

After the Germans took over southern France in November 1942, Stosskopf had to find another means of communicating with the Allies. He eventually hooked up with the British through the "Alliance" network (also known as "Noah's Ark," because of the agents' animal code names) run by Marie-Madeleine Fourcade in southern France. Fourcade had aligned herself with General Henri-Honoré Giraud, Charles De Gaulle's rival for control of the Free French movement. Stosskopf was run separately from Fourcade's other agents and only loosely connected with the network, however.

This was fortunate: Fourcade's amateurs were only barely able to cope with the Vichy police and proved to be easy pickings for the Gestapo. When the Germans occupied southern France, the Alliance network was destroyed inside of a year.

Stosskopf held out until early 1944, and continued his intelligence reports (at considerable risk) through some unknown link to the Anglo-American intelligence services. He was finally caught on February 21, 1944, however, and sent to the Struthoff concentration camp in the Vosges mountains, where he was executed on September 1, 1944.

resistance tended to be passive but was often quite effective. In 1944, the Danish people managed to save most of the country's 6,000 Jews from the Holocaust in a groundswell of unparalleled popular support. Some 5,500 people were taken from under the noses of the Gestapo and spirited across the Danish Straits into neutral Sweden. In the end, the Nazis managed to round up only 472 people, mainly those who could not be rescued in time or who were too sick or too old to move.

In Yugoslavia, the SOE at first supported Mihailovich's royalist Chetnik movement, but then switched to Tito's communist partisans, thereby keeping them independent of Moscow. Both groups had been effective in playing the German and Italian occupying forces against each other. They also fought tenaciously against the Nazi-backed Ustashe movement that established itself in Croatia and in the ethnically diverse provinces of Bosnia and Herzegovina. By 1943, they had so eroded the strength of the Ustashe that its leader, Ante Pavelich, was hailed in Berlin as the mayor of Zagreb—because that was all the territory he really controlled. The Titoist victory in 1945 meant only that the hatred generated by all this infighting was driven underground, where it simmered for nearly fifty years, only to burst forth again at the end of the Cold War.

Allied-sponsored resistance in east Asia was hindered by the legacy of colonial repression, but the British supplied active guerilla movements in Malaya and Burma with arms and supplies, while also running arms to both Ch'iang Kai-shek and Mao Ze-Dong in China. The Americans supported Ho Chi Minh's nationalist resistance movement in Vietnam, while stranded regular American and Filipino troops formed a hard core of resistance in the Philippines.

But, in general, the resistance achieved few decisive results. Resistance forces were an annoyance to the occupiers, in that they caused damage and casualties and were a constant drain on morale, but it is debatable whether, with a few noteworthy exceptions, they achieved anything more concrete than tying down extra troops at garrisons (most of which were second-line units anyway, and ill-suited to regular combat roles). Their main achievement was to keep hope alive, and to remind the enemy that the war had not yet been won.

LEFT: Waging a never-ending guerilla war against the German troops occupying France, the French maquis achieved some dramatic successes, as this destroyed train might suggest. But German reprisals were always swift and ruthless, and the destruction of a single train could result in the execution of a dozen or more innocent people. BELOW: Worse was the work of French collaborators, who worked with the SS to root out the maquis, settling old scores in the process. Here, two members of the fascist French Militia interrogate a man suspected of being in the resistance.

# The Double-Cross System

Easily the most successful counterintelligence operation of World War II, and perhaps of all time, the double-cross system was run by the XX-committee (XX, as in twenty), a sub-unit of MI-5, or British counterintelligence. Headed by John C. Masterman, the XX-committee was formed to control German espionage penetration of the United Kingdom. Rather than simply arresting spies as they were uncovered, however, the XX-committee "turned" them: that is, they left them in place, to be run as double agents. The British then used the "double-cross system," as it was known, to pass disinformation (false information) to the enemy. In every other respect, the XX-committee double agents continued to function as if they were active German spies. With MI-5's help, many of them even recruited and ran their own subnetworks, thereby

# WARNING
## from the
# FBI

**The war against spies and saboteurs demands the aid of every American.**

**When you see evidence of sabotage, notify the Federal Bureau of Investigation at once.**

**When you suspect the presence of enemy agents, tell it to the FBI.**

**Beware of those who spread enemy propaganda!** __Don't repeat vicious rumors or vicious whispers.__

**Tell it to the FBI!**

J. Edgar Hoover, *Director*
*Federal Bureau of Investigation*

The nearest Federal Bureau of Investigation office is listed on page one of your telephone directory.

ACCIDENT OR SABOTAGE?

PREVENT IT BY VIGILANCE

CONSOLIDATED EDISON SYSTEM COMPANIES

ABOVE: Although German agents had waged a successful sabotage war against the United States during World War I, they consistently failed in similar efforts during World War II. These two FBI posters mark the vigilance of U.S. wartime security.

enhancing their value as agents both for the Abwehr and British intelligence. Most important, all these agents continued to be paid by the Germans; in fact, XX-committee operations were largely financed by the Abwehr.

Even though it was fairly obvious that MI-5 had completely subverted the German espionage network in the United Kingdom, the XX-committee operated on the assumption that there were other German agents at large who might not be under their control and might provide the Germans with a means of checking the disinformation provided by the growing networks of British-controlled double agents. British success in penetrating the German ENIGMA codes, which gave them more or less complete access to German intelligence communications, helped immeasurably.

Each XX-committee agent was assigned a case officer who was intimately familiar with the agent and carefully monitored every aspect of his or her life. The XX-committee meticulously crafted the intelligence that agents fed to the Germans and constantly checked for internal consistency and believability. Beginning in 1942, XX-comittee resources were largely focused on the highly successful deception operations that were part of the plans for the invasion of Normandy (see "Operation Fortitude," in Chapter 7). Indeed, the XX-committee's success at deception was absolute: the Germans never stumbled on the truth, or even guessed that they were being deceived.

Perhaps the most successful MI-5 double agent was Dusko Popov (code name "Tricycle"), a Yugoslav lawyer who was approached by the Abwehr to spy on

# Operation Pastorius

In World War I, German saboteurs had operated extensively throughout North America, attacking British-owned firms and targets related to the Allied war effort. Their most notorious enterprise was the destruction of a large quantity of munitions stored at a warehouse on Black Tom Island in New York Harbor.

By comparison, German espionage in the United States during World War II was stunningly inept. Despite a sinister reputation (partly built on experience from the previous war) German attempts to build up networks in the United States prior to the outbreak of war were completely unsuccessful. With the aid of a double agent, William G. Sebold, the FBI was able to put virtually the entire German espionage apparatus out of action by June 1940.

In 1942, the Abwehr tried to recover from this serious setback. Eight saboteurs were recruited from among Germans who had lived in the United States prior to the war and had returned to Germany after September 1939. All were archetypal Nazis from lower middle-class backgrounds who had worked in various service or artisanal positions in the United States during the 1930s.

The plan was to put two teams of four agents ashore from U-boats on the East Coast of the United States: one on Long Island, the other on the coast of Florida. The teams were to work their way inland and attack Eastern Seaboard and Midwest aluminum manufacturing plants that were vital to aircraft production.

The plan went awry from the very beginning. On the night of June 12, 1942, the New York team landed on Long Island. They were immediately sighted by a young Coast Guardsman, John Cullen, whom they first attempted to fool with a story about their being fishermen, and then tried to bribe. Being outnumbered and sensing that he was in danger, Cullen let them go but reported the incident and turned in the money. Nonetheless, within twenty-four hours the team had gone to ground in New York City.

At this point, the team leader, Georg J. Dasch (who for eighteen years had been a waiter in New York and San Francisco) panicked. Identifying himself as Franz Daniel Pastorius he walked into the FBI office in New York and spilled the beans on the whole operation. By the end of the month, all the would-be saboteurs were in the hands of the authorities. Dasch and another team member, Ernst P. Burger (who was complicit in his betrayal of his comrades) were given stiff prison sentences. The other six team members were sentenced to death and immediately executed. In 1948 Dasch and Burger were deported to Germany.

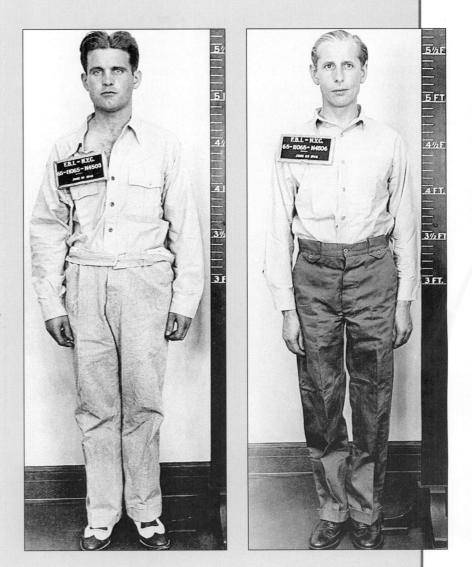

Would-be German saboteurs Eduard Kerling (left) and Georg Dasch (right) as they appeared in the FBI mug shots. Each lead a team of four agents put ashore by U-boat in 1942, with plans to wander about the United States blowing up aluminum plants and aircraft factories. Dasch, who was landed in Long Island, blew the whole operation when he turned himself in to the FBI office in New York. Acting on his information, the FBI immediately arrested the rest of his team and tracked down Kerling's agents, who had just been landed in Florida. Dasch and another team member, Ernest Burger, who also helped the authorities, were rewarded with long prison sentences—the others were summarily executed.

German efforts to infiltrate the United Kingdom during World War II were often stunningly inept. Karel Richter (pictured here with his British "minders") was dropped into England by parachute early in 1941 and arrested shortly after he landed. A Sudeten German, he spoke only broken English and did not know how to use the wireless transmitter his superiors had given him. His mission was to see if Wulf Schmidt (British code name Tate), another German agent already in England, was under British control (he was). Richter also brought a spare crystal to repair Schmidt's wireless transmitter, but the crystal did not fit. Richter's contact in England, Arthur George Evans (Snow) was also working for the British, as were all of Germany's other agents in the United Kingdom. Richter, too incompetent to be useful, was shot as a spy, as was Joseph Jakobs, another German agent who arrived by parachute in 1941. Unfortunately for Jakobs, his arrest was discovered and reported in the press, which made it impossible to use him as a double agent.

the British in 1940, while his country was still neutral. Armed with this information, Popov immediately went to British intelligence, who was able to persuade him to operate as a double agent. Popov next went to Lisbon as the representative of a consortium of Yugoslav banks. For most of the next year, he traveled the world working for the Abwehr—and MI-5. In August 1941, the Germans sent him to the United States to set up a network to report on economic and military matters. Once in the United States, however, Tricycle came under the purview of J. Edgar Hoover's FBI who, by arrangement with MI-5, ran Popov as an agent in North America. Unfortunately, Hoover disliked and distrusted Popov intensely. As a result, the FBI so botched the job that it raised Abwehr suspicions. Popov returned to the United Kingdom in October 1942 and managed to reestablish

his credentials with the Germans. Soon he was deeply imbedded in Operation Fortitude. He also succeeded in extracting some £20,000 from the Abwehr. After the war Popov was decorated by the British and made a British subject.

Tricycle was unusual in that he was a volunteer and had a certain amount of credibility from the very beginning. Another volunteer was the Spaniard Juan Pujol ("Garbo"), who first tricked the Abwehr into believing that he was sending them messages from Great Britain (he was actually in Lisbon), then offered himself to the British. Garbo and his case officer concocted a network of some fourteen subagents to disseminate disinformation of various kinds to the Germans. Like Tricycle, Garbo's major function was to disseminate disinformation concerning the planned invasion of Normandy. He

LEFT: A German agent sent into the United States in 1941, Frederick Duquesne was betrayed to the FBI by double agent William G. Sebold. Duquesne had a large organization of at least 33 agents. All were arrested before the United States entered the war. BELOW LEFT: Some of the communications equipment smuggled into the United States by the Duquesne spy ring.

was so successful in this activity that he was decorated twice: by the British, with an MBE, and by the Germans, with the Iron Cross.

Most other double agents operated under at least a minimal amount of coercion. Arthur George Evans ("Snow"), for example, was planted by the Abwehr in the 1930s and operated under the threat of arrest. Wulf Schmidt ("Tate") was a Danish Nazi who was para-chuted into Britain in September 1940. Snow and other double agents helped MI-5 track down the nascent German network in Great Britain. By the end of the year, MI-5 was reasonably certain that they had located all the German agents. The one exception, Jan Ter Braak, committed suicide in April 1941. Incredibly, despite some close calls, the double-cross system func-tioned right up to the end of the war.

# Chapter 4

# Intelligence in the Pacific War

IN THE FIRST HALF OF THE TWENTIETH CENTURY, THE JAPANESE EMPIRE WAS AN aggressive, expansionist power that had managed to conquer Korea, Manchuria, and large sections of China. In 1937, Japan launched a full-scale invasion of China and rapidly overran most of the country. Japan failed to decisively defeat the Chinese army, however, and soon found itself bogged down in a war it could not win.

The West knew little about Japan in the 1930s: a closed, quasifeudal society, it was dominated by a powerful military elite that viewed all foreigners with suspicion and imposed a veil of secrecy that was difficult for Westerners to penetrate. Deprived not only of attaché reporting but also of secret agents, both the British and American intelligence services were forced to rely almost exclusively on signals intelligence. By 1939 the Singapore-based British Far Eastern Combined Bureau (FECB) had penetrated most Japanese diplomatic, attaché, and naval ciphers, only to lose them all when the Japanese switched to their version of the ENIGMA machine. The Americans were reading PURPLE, the new Japanese diplomatic cipher and also the main Japanese naval cipher, JN-25, until the end of 1940, but lost that source of information when the Imperial Navy shifted to the ENIGMA-based JN-25B.

The imperfect picture thus available to the West showed a Japan with ambitions that far surpassed her capabilities. The China quagmire, in

The American aircraft carrier *Lexington* burns after a Japanese attack during the Battle of the Coral Sea. The *Lexington* was sunk and the aircraft carrier *Yorktown* was heavily damaged, but not before wreaking enough havoc for the Japanese to call off the attack.

particular, seemed to be overtaxing Japanese resources by demanding ever-increasing commitments—much as would happen to the United States in Vietnam twenty-five years later. In December 1939, FECB was encouraged when it intercepted a telegram from the Japanese foreign minister to Berlin that stressed the importance of ending the war in China and avoiding confrontation with Great Britain and France. But a split between Japan's army and navy over China made it difficult to decipher Japanese intentions.

All the same, Whitehall and Washington became increasingly alarmed about Japanese policy. The fear was that the defeat of France and Britain's continued preoccupation with the war in Europe would create irresistible opportunities in Asia for the Japanese leadership. Tension increased over the summer of 1940 when the Japanese pressured the Dutch colonial administration in the East Indies to increase supplies of tin and oil. Japanese troops then occupied bases in northern French Indochina. In December 1940, signals intelligence showed Thai Prime Minister Pibul Songgram cooperating with the Japanese in exchange for territorial claims in Laos and Cambodia. This opened the back door to Malaya and Britain's main Asian naval base, Singapore. In September 1940, Japan had joined the European Axis. Over the course of the following year, there was increased evidence of close cooperation with Nazi Germany (including in intelligence matters) as well as evidence that Japan was mobilizing for a long war. That Japan was set on war seemed certain in September 1941, when the militant general Tojo Hideki was made prime minister.

Incredibly, the only solution the Japanese could find to bring an end to the fighting in China was to widen the already intractable war—again, much like the United States a quarter-century later in Vietnam. Tokyo believed that the only way to defeat China was to cut off all outside aid. The army wanted to drive north, severing China's ties with the Soviet Union. The navy favored a "southern" solution that would cut China off from the rest of the world while securing needed supplies of oil and tin through conquest of the Dutch East Indies.

The northern option was closed off when the Soviets decisively defeated the Japanese army in a series of border clashes at Kalkhin-Gol, after which Japan

LEFT: President Roosevelt meets with British Prime Minister Winston S. Churchill aboard the British battleship *Prince of Wales* in Argentia Bay, on the coast of Newfoundland. Here, Roosevelt shakes hands with the captain of the *Prince of Wales*, John C. Leach. Churchill is behind Leach, to his left. A few months later, the *Prince of Wales* was sunk and Leach drowned in a Japanese bomber attack in the South China Sea. But the partnership forged in Argentia Bay—which among other things included intelligence cooperation—helped bring victory to the Allies in World War II. FOLLOWING PAGE: A Japanese map of Pearl Harbor, including battleship row, with the location of the American battleships provided by an agent.

negotiated a neutrality pact with Moscow. But in June 1941, Germany invaded the Soviet Union, and Japan had to decide whether to support its German allies or take advantage of the situation to move into Southeast Asia. In July, the cabinet and military leaders opted to move south.

The foundation for Japanese strategy was a plan worked out by the Imperial Combined Fleet Staff, under Admiral Yamamoto Isoroku. Yamamoto planned a preemptive strike against the U.S. Pacific Fleet at Pearl Harbor, using the Japanese Navy's six attack carriers. Meanwhile, invasion forces would set out for the Dutch East Indies and U.S. possessions in the Pacific: Wake Island, Guam, and most important, the Philippines. An overland invasion force would march south out of Thailand into Malaya to take the main British naval base at Singapore. This attack would be supported by a powerful force of battleships and heavy cruisers, along with air striking forces based in Indochina. Another land force would take Burma and threaten India. The main Japanese battle fleet—including six of Japan's ten battleships—would remain in home waters, ready to take on the remnants of the U.S. fleet if it sortied across the Pacific. The whole plan was a shoestring operation that stretched Japanese resources to the utmost. It was also a terrific gamble. But Yamamoto, who had served in the United States, knew how to calculate Western reactions better than his contemporaries in Japan did. He also understood the ultimate futility of a Japanese-American war. When asked what he thought the prospects for success were, he prophesied that Japan would "run wild" for six months but, after that, "I have utterly no confidence."

British and American intelligence analysts watched these developments from afar with growing unease. In November 1940 the United States took the almost unprecedented step of sharing the breakthrough into Japanese diplomatic codes (MAGIC) with the British. The Japanese naval code, JN-25B, remained difficult to penetrate, but American cryptographers were working around the clock. The British FECB in Singapore did manage to plot some Japanese fleet movements, as did a small Dutch cryptanalysis unit in Java, but the code became unreadable again on the eve of war when the Japanese introduced additional encryption. MAGIC

nonetheless continued to provide important information, especially as the countdown to war began.

Over June and July 1941, MAGIC revealed the pressure the Japanese were applying to the French colonial administration in Indochina and gave warning of their occupation of southern Vietnam, Laos, and Cambodia. Other signals showed Japanese consuls seeking intelligence on the defenses of the Dutch East Indies. On November 19, 1941, a MAGIC intercept identified a Japanese code message to be transmitted in the event of a rupture of diplomatic relations with the United States: EAST WIND RAIN. Just three days later, the Japanese foreign minister, Togo Shigenori, warned the Japanese ambassador in Washington, Nomura Kichasaburo, that he had until the end of the month to negotiate a settlement with the United States. "After that," read the message, "things are automatically going to happen." More ominous still was an unscheduled change in Imperial Navy ship call signs, the kind of step that betokened war. Finally, Japanese agents were detected reporting on U.S. military dispositions and the number, type, and positioning of U.S. warships in harbor. In general, the available evidence convinced Washington that war was imminent, but U.S. officials simply failed to become alert to the possibility of an attack on the U.S. Pacific Fleet in Pearl Harbor. Rather, the activities of Japanese agents convinced both Washington and the local military commanders that the real danger was from sabotage—this despite a number of war games and prewar exercises that signaled the threat of a carrier strike on Pearl, just as it was to occur. After the attack, this inability to coordinate and evaluate information in context was one of the reasons given for the creation of the Central Intelligence Agency after World War II.

In truth, the structure of the Japanese attack made a strike on the Hawaiian Islands difficult to predict. Although the Japanese carriers left to take up positions north of Hawaii on November 22, 1941, they maintained strict radio silence, and were therefore impossible to locate, barring a chance sighting by aircraft or shipping vessels. American and British intelligence analysts correctly interpreted the available intelligence on Japanese naval movements as foreshadowing an attack on the British and Dutch possessions in Southeast Asia.

Additional MAGIC intelligence showed Japanese legations burning their files in Manila, Djakarta, Singapore, and Hong Kong, as well as in Washington and London. Because he was told to anticipate war, the U.S. Pacific Fleet commander, Admiral Husband Kimmel, sent his carrier commander, Vice Admiral William F. Halsey, to reinforce Wake Island with Marine F4F Wildcat fighters. Halsey had delivered his fighters and was on his way back to the base at Pearl Harbor when the Japanese carried out their attack. Thus, although the Japanese striking force took out the American battle fleet, the attack missed the carriers, a chance failure that would cost the Japanese Navy very dearly.

In the meantime, Admiral Yamamoto performed as promised. In Singapore, the British were surprised by the speed of the Japanese advance. For their part, the Japanese were concerned about the presence of the new battleship *Prince of Wales* and the battle cruiser *Repulse,* powerful units that overmatched anything the Japanese had in the area. To the surprise of both sides, however, the two capital ships were caught by Japanese torpedo bombers off the Malayan coast and sunk on December 10. Singapore was soon besieged, and it was surrendered on February 15, 1942. Over the next few weeks, Japanese forces overran Hong Kong, the Philippines, the Dutch East Indies, Burma, and the American possessions in the Pacific.

With British and American fortunes at their lowest ebb, intelligence breakthroughs helped the Allies redress the situation. With Allied forces scattered and defeated all over the Pacific, it became imperative for the Allies to know where the Japanese would strike next. The only way to find this out was to break the Japanese naval codes. Commonwealth units on Ceylon (modern-day Sri Lanka) and in Australia, plus U.S. Naval code-breaking units in Washington and at Pearl itself, all bent themselves to the task, working around the clock.

Although the Allies could read only 12 to 15 percent of Japanese signals, in March 1942 the head of the Pearl Harbor unit, Commander Joseph Rochefort, correctly deduced a coming Japanese move on New Guinea. Further intercepts in April supported that contention, and Admiral Chester W. Nimitz, the new commander-in-chief of the Pacific Fleet (CinCPac,)

TOP: An aerial shot shows Hickam Field burning after the Japanese attack on Pearl Harbor. The naval and military commanders in Hawaii were mostly concerned about sabotage and concentrated their aircraft to better protect them from attack by non-existent Japanese agents. Thus the planes were easy targets for the carrier strikes when they came. BOTTOM: A Japanese torpedo bomber climbs away from the burning Pearl Harbor preparatory to returning to its carrier. Although Western intelligence knew the Japanese were about to go to war, they failed to anticipate a carrier strike on Hawaii.

The British warships *Prince of Wales* and *Repulse* maneuver to avoid bombs being dropped by high-flying Japanese twin-engine bombers in the South China Sea. The speed and effectiveness with which these attacks were carried out shocked the British, who had greatly underrated Japanese capabilities.

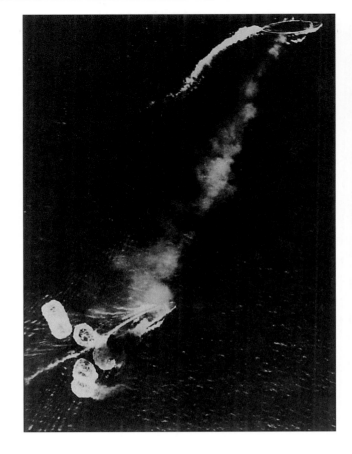

dispatched the aircraft carriers *Lexington* and *Yorktown* to the Southwest Pacific. There, they engaged a Japanese carrier force in the Battle of the Coral Sea. *Lexington* was sunk and the *Yorktown* heavily damaged, but the Japanese lost the light carrier *Riujo* and suffered damage to the brand-new fleet carrier, *Shokaku*. Most important, however, the American force mauled the *Shokaku*'s air group as well as that of her sister ship, *Zuikaku*. Neither carrier would be available for the Battle of Midway the following June. Finally, the Japanese were forced to cancel their invasion of New Guinea, which would have given them air bases from which to attack Australia and the Solomon Islands.

By now, the Allies were reading a substantial portion of Japanese naval communications. These were providing ample evidence of a new attack planned for somewhere in the Central Pacific. Messages were broken from Japanese warships requesting replenishment hoses used in mid-ocean refueling and maps of the Aleutians and the waters around Hawaii. Plans for

The British battleship *Prince of Wales* arrives in Singapore on December 2, 1941. Dispatched—along with the battle cruiser *Repulse*— in the hope of deterring Japanese attack, the *Prince of Wales* was Britain's newest battleship. Eight days later, she and the *Repulse* were sunk after being subjected to six separate attacks by 85 Japanese bombers.

# Fatal Underestimation of a Deadly Enemy

In the decades before World War II, Japan was widely regarded as a second-rate military power. Many Westerners seriously believed that the Japanese had some genetic defect that prevented them from being good pilots. Others sought refuge in cultural stereotypes: the warrior code called *Bushido*, for example, was acknowledged to value personal bravery, but was thought to discourage independent thought in favor of reckless self-sacrifice. Forgotten were the bloody defeats inflicted on the (albeit corrupt and poorly led) Imperial Russian army in the Russo-Japanese War, along with Admiral Togo Heihachiro's cool annihilation of the Imperial Russian Baltic Fleet in 1905, at the time admired as a model victory.

What was true was that the Japan of the 1930s was not equipped to wage a modern, mechanized war against a major industrial power and did not have the resources to sustain a lengthy continental war such as the one it had launched in China. Japanese armies inflicted formidable defeats on the Chinese army (admittedly not a highly regarded military force itself), but were consistently unable to decisively defeat it in the field. The Japanese armies themselves were savagely mauled by Soviet troops in a series of border clashes that erupted around Kalkhin-Gol. On August 14, 1937, obsolete Chinese fighters inflicted between 30 percent and 50 percent casualties on attacking Japanese aircraft over Nanking and Shanghai, a victory still celebrated in China as Chinese Air Force Day.

Watching these defeats, Western observers missed the very real qualities of Japanese aircraft such as the G3M2 Type 96 bomber (given the Allied code name "Nell"): speed, endurance, and high carrying capacity. The G3M2 was widely believed to be a copy of the greatly inferior Junkers Ju-86, an aircraft rejected by the Luftwaffe that Junkers had attempted to sell to Japan in 1935. Although mid-1930s Japanese fighters possibly were inferior to contemporary Western designs, the next generation—the army's Ki-27 (Nate) and the navy's A5M4 (Claude)—considerably shortened whatever lead the West had. Westerners also sneered at the unusual design of Japanese warships, missing the development of the fearsome Type 93 Long-Lance torpedo, a weapon twice as powerful, twice as fast, and twice as long-ranged as anything in the Anglo-American arsenal. Western intelligence also was totally ignorant of the true characteristics of the Yamato-class battleships—the largest ever built—then under construction in Japanese shipyards.

The veil of secrecy hung over Japan by its leaders also worked to keep true Japanese capabilities secret. In 1940 and 1941, the Japanese deployed a whole new generation of aircraft, including the famous A6M2 Type 0 fighter—the Zero, known officially to the Allies as "Zeke"—and the fast and powerful G4M2 Type 1 bomber (Betty). The British in particular knew nothing of these aircraft when war broke out and, in reinforcing the fighters of the Singapore garrison, had opted for the American-built Brewster B-339 Buffalo, an aircraft perhaps suited to take on the Nates and Claudes of the previous generation of Japanese aircraft, but nearly helpless against the deadly Zeros.

The Japanese military had its moment of truth in December 1941. Westerners were forced to fall back in disarray before the stunning, swiftly executed attacks of the same Japanese who, just weeks before, had been held in thinly veiled contempt by Western observers.

Western intelligence observers considered the Japanese A5M4 Type 96 fighter (above), or "Claude," as it was known, to be typical of Japanese aircraft in 1941. Although a good aircraft in its day, the Claude was obsolete and was being phased out of service by the time the Japanese launched the Pacific War. In its stead, the Allies found themselves opposed by the deadly Japanese "Zero" fighter.

LEFT: The tubby Brewster B-339 Buffalo fighters supplied to the British and Dutch air forces in Southeast Asia were well equipped to take on the previous generation of Japanese aircraft—such as the Claude—but were hopelessly outclassed by the Zero. BELOW: The Zero was better than any Allied fighter in the Pacific at the outbreak of war.

Japan's Admiral Yamamoto Isoroku, architect of the attack on Pearl Harbor and Japanese naval Commander-in-Chief for the first year and a half of war. Almost alone among Japan's leaders, Yamamoto did not underestimate American war potential. He promised simply to "run wild" for six months; after that, he said, "I have utterly no confidence."

reconnaissance of Hawaii were detected. A new designator—"AF"—kept appearing, which Rochefort guessed referred to the target.

By now CinCPac was convinced that the target was Midway. To confirm this, a deception plan was devised: by secure communications, Midway was ordered to report by wireless that its fresh-water plant was out of operation and to urgently request parts. A few days later, a Japanese signal was intercepted indicating that AF was out of fresh water. CinCPac now knew the secret.

On May 27, 1942, Yamamoto and the main Japanese battle fleet left for the island of Midway while a smaller force mounted a diversionary attack on the Aleutian Islands. With Yamamoto were four of Japan's fleet carriers. Waiting for him was Black Jack Fletcher with the carriers *Enterprise*, *Hornet*, and the miraculously repaired *Yorktown*. Among other things, knowing the place of the attack had given the repair yard at Pearl Harbor the chance to turn the damaged carrier around in record time. For his part, Yamamoto was sure that he had achieved surprise, and he believed that the *Yorktown* was sunk. On June 6, he was disabused of these notions when his four carriers were attacked and sunk. The Imperial Japanese Navy (IJN) also lost about 300 highly trained pilots, a loss from which they never recovered. The U.S. Navy lost the carrier *Yorktown*, but the invasion force was turned back. It was six months since the attack on Pearl Harbor, almost to the day.

Two days later, the IJN changed its codes, and the JN-25B became unreadable until the end of 1942. The U.S. Navy thus fought the ferocious battles off Guadalcanal without the benefit of comprehensive signals intelligence. By 1943, JN-25B was again broken, and it generally remained readable until the end of the war.

For Admiral Yamamoto, a last encounter with Western cryptanalysis came the following year. In April 1943, Allied cryptanalysts picked up a message giving the exact itinerary of the Japanese leader's planned inspection trip to the Solomon Islands. P-38 fighters were dispatched to shoot down the G4M2 bomber in which he was flying, and he was killed.

The American carrier *Lexington* explodes and sinks after the Battle of the Coral Sea. This was the first action in which Allied penetration of the Japanese JN25B naval code allowed them to anticipate Japanese moves in the Pacific War. Although the U.S. Navy suffered greater losses than the Japanese in this action, they rebounded quickly and were able to meet and defeat the Japanese carrier force at Midway.

# Chapter 5

# The War in the Mediterranean

THE MEDITERRANEAN WAS QUIET UNTIL JUNE 1940, WHEN BENITO MUSSOLINI, Italy's fascist dictator, brought his country into the war in an ill-judged effort to be at Hitler's side when Great Britain and France surrendered. Italy was in no way prepared for war. The Italian army was largely unmechanized; the air force was highly efficient, but obsolescent and in the midst of a program of modernization. The navy was also an effective force, but it was small and technologically behind the times. Four powerful new battleships were nearing completion, but the surface forces lacked both aircraft carriers and an adequate force of land-based naval aircraft, not to mention effective antisubmarine weapons. Moreover, the naval high command (*Supermarina*) was acutely aware that the Italian navy had not fought an active war since 1859, when they had been soundly defeated by the Austrian navy. They also knew that in a long war, there would be no way to replace any losses. Faced with England's powerful Royal Navy, Italian admirals thus tended to be very cautious and reluctant to commit their precious warships to action.

The war began badly for Italy. An offensive into southern France stagnated after the Italians ran into stiff resistance from the French, even though the French were nearly prostrate after the devastating German assault the previous month. In North Africa, Marshal Rudolfo Graziani, the governor of Libya (then an Italian colony), lurched across the border into Egypt (a British protectorate) the following September,

Victory in North Africa hinged on supplies. Despite heavy losses, the Italian navy brought in supply convoys carrying major reinforcements, such as this powerful Pkzw VI Tiger tank. But for every Tiger in North Africa, there were a dozen Churchill infantry tanks, such as the one seen in the background.

only to halt along the coast, reluctant to proceed any farther without motorized transport. The following month, Mussolini sent his army into Greece, only to be mauled by the Greek army, defending in the mountains. Winter soon came, and with it a Greek counterattack that not only drove the Italians out of Greece, but seemed likely to expel them from the Balkans altogether.

The British forces in the Mediterranean were smaller than those deployed by the Italians, but better trained and more experienced. The Mediterranean Fleet, under Sir Andrew Cunningham, had been drawn down somewhat over 1939 and 1940 to reinforce the Atlantic Fleet, but was quickly reinforced with modern aircraft carriers and powerful, modernized battleships. At Gibraltar was another fleet, "Force H," commanded by Sir James Somerville, which stood poised either to fight in the western Mediterranean or to steam out into the Atlantic. The British army in Egypt, under Sir Archibald Wavell, was small but highly mobile and well-adapted to desert conditions. Most important, it included the Seventh Armored Division (the "Desert Rats") and a battalion

of powerful infantry tanks (the famous Matildas), which were slow but well able to defeat the few Italian tanks and impervious to anything the Italians could throw at them (except heavy artillery).

The British counteroffensive began in November 1940. On the night of November 11, twenty-one Swordfish torpedo bombers, flying off the armored aircraft carrier *Illustrious*, staged a night attack on the main Italian fleet at its base at Taranto, a tactic at which the British excelled. Photo reconnaissance and signals intelligence had showed where the barrage balloons and torpedo nets were deployed and had showed the attackers how to avoid the few anti-aircraft guns available to the Italians. Three battleships were put out of action (one of them permanently) and a heavy cruiser was damaged. In one stroke, the Italian navy had been neutralized, a defeat from which Supermarina failed to recover until the following March. On December 9, 1940, in the North African desert, the British field commander, Sir Richard O'Conner, used his tanks to surround and capture the bulk of Graziani's much larger but nearly immobile forces and

The British aircraft carrier *Illustrious*, crippled by German Ju-87 dive bombers, or Stukas, as they were called. The presence of German dive bomber units in the Mediterranean took the British completely by surprise. Always quick to underestimate their Italian opponents, they never realized the important role played by Italian dive bomber units—flying German-supplied Ju-87s—in attacks on British warships and convoys.

In the trackless wastes of the Western Desert, communications and intelligence were of paramount importance. Both sides used irregular forces, such as these British commandos, to wreak havoc behind enemy lines and disrupt communications—and also to collect intelligence.

drive the remnants of his army back to his base at Tripoli. The Italians had now been defeated on every front in which they were engaged and it looked very much as if Mussolini's Italy was to be driven out of the war.

The run of Italian defeats brought German intervention. Hitler, in particular, was enraged by Mussolini's incompetent conduct of the war and concerned that continued Italian defeats would expose the southern German flank—especially the important oil fields at Ploesti in Romania—to attack. Over the winter of 1940 to 1941, OKW, the German High Command, diverted forces being assembled for the Russian campaign into the Balkans for a lightning campaign against Greece and Yugoslavia. In February and March, a small force, comprising two divisions (the Fifteenth Panzer and the Fifth light [mechanized], soon to be expanded and renamed the Twenty-first Panzer) and supporting units, was transported to Tripoli (Operation Sonnenblume) to

shore up the crumbling Italian position in Libya. Hitler gave this small force the somewhat dramatic name of *Deutsches Afrika Korps*. Its commander was soon to become a household name: Erwin Rommel.

Up until then, intelligence had played only an unspectacular supporting role in the Mediterranean. Now it was to become central to both Allied and Axis operations, and both sides were to benefit enormously from their respective strengths in this area. ULTRA undoubtedly gave the British the advantage in the long run, but the overall situation accentuated German strengths in battlefield reconnaissance and signals intelligence. Moreover, Rommel was fortunate in his choice of staff intelligence officer, Major Friedrich Wilhelm von Mellenthin, and he had a priceless asset in the armored cars and equipment of the Third Radio Intercept Company (*Horchkompanie*), commanded by Leutnant Alfred Seebohm. For the next year or so, until it was

decimated and captured during the fighting at the first Battle of El Alamein, this unit provided Rommel with up-to-the-minute reporting on the movements and dispositions of Allied military forces. It was this kind of intelligence that enabled the "Desert Fox" to build his reputation for tactical brilliance and intuitive genius on the battlefield.

In addition, beginning in the winter of 1941 to 1942, Rommel had a source literally inside the Allied High Command. In August 1941, Italian military intelligence, SIM, had succeeded in obtaining a copy of the code used by the U.S. military attaché in Cairo, Colonel Bonner Frank Fellers. Fellers had access to the most sensitive military secrets and regularly made reports about British conduct of the war, even noting their intentions or plans for attack. These were routinely read by SIM and the results passed immediately to Rommel. Thus the Germans frequently knew British plans even before the commanders in the field were privy to them. (See "The Good Source," page 77.)

Finally, the Germans had a valuable intelligence asset in the Desert Fox himself. Rommel was not a good intelligence target, particularly for signals intelligence. He was arrogant, supremely self-confident, and headstrong. He routinely disobeyed orders. In his own signals, he frequently exaggerated his own strengths and/or

ABOVE: German Panzer troops inspect a knocked-out British Matilda infantry tank. The heavily armored Matildas devastated Italian armored forces in 1940, but were overmatched by German tanks such as this 21st Panzer Division Pzkw III G, fitted with bolt-on applique armor. Rommel's greatest strengths, however, lay in his superior tactical intelligence units and his own unpredictability, which went a long way toward compensating for Allied intelligence successes, especially in the winter of 1941 to 1942. OPPOSITE: Operating in an unusual role, American B-25 Mitchell bombers attack German Ju-52 transports en route to North Africa. Allied penetration of the Axis Enigma signals enabled them to locate and intercept formations such as this one, bringing in troops. The German transports often flew at low levels to avoid radar detection.

Allied supplies had to come all the way around North Africa, a very long distance, and often were slow in coming. But, even at the height of the U-boat war, they were reasonably secure. Here, an American-built M3 Grant tank is loaded onto a ship bound for Alexandria.

When Rommel and the Deutsches Afrika Korps arrived in Tripoli beginning in February 1941, Wavell was given to believe from signals intercepts that the German commander's role was to be limited to shoring up the Italian position in Libya. Offensive operations were strictly forbidden. He thus acceded to Prime Minister Winston Churchill's incessant prodding to send troops to Greece to forestall the German attack that ULTRA told the British was coming in the Balkans.

But Rommel's tactical signals intelligence units detected the withdrawal of British troops. Instead of doing as he was told, Rommel drove out into the desert that April, retaking Libya, encircling the British forces in the "bulge" of Cyrenaica, and besieging the British fortress of Tobruk (which the British had taken from the Italian army just a few months before). An assault by Rommel on Tobruk was repulsed, but with heavy losses. Meanwhile, the British were expelled from Greece by the German invasion and thrown out of Crete after a brief but bloody battle. Cunningham's Mediterranean Fleet managed to evacuate most of the British troops from Crete, but only at the cost of many lives.

In Berlin, the chief of the German General Staff, General Franz Halder, sent an armored warfare expert, Friedrich von Paulus, to North Africa to try to restrain Rommel, who was dangerously overextended and low on supplies. Convinced that he had talked sense into Rommel, Paulus sent a signal to Berlin via Luftwaffe ENIGMA that outlined Rommel's weaknesses and his instructions to hold his position and advance no further. In receipt of Paulus' signal and reinforced by tanks rushed through the Mediterranean, Wavell was encouraged to attack, with Churchill's blessing. Once again, Rommel's superior battlefield signals intelligence warned him of British plans. Betrayed by poor radio security, both Operations Brevity and Battleaxe were repulsed in rapid succession by the Deutsches Afrika Korps. Both sides were now exhausted and dug in for the summer and fall of 1941. In Cairo, Wavell was replaced as Middle East commander by the British commander-in-chief in India, Field Marshal Sir Claude Auchinleck.

"The Auk," as he was known, immediately began gearing up for a winter offensive, Operation Crusader. In the meantime, the Royal Navy struck at Rommel's

underestimated those of the enemy to deliberately mislead his own superiors. Sometimes he simply lied. In consequence, he was hated and mistrusted by OKW and the German General Staff in Berlin, who were constantly reprimanding him or trying to rein him in. The signals traffic that this kind of behavior generated was confusing and frequently misled Allied intelligence officers, who often had grandstand seats (via ULTRA) to the contretemps between North Africa and Berlin.

# The Good Source: Colonel Bonner Frank Fellers

Italian military intelligence was adept at cryptanalysis, but the SIM's real specialty was physically stealing the codes other countries used for their secret communications. By such methods, Mussolini's spies had penetrated most of the diplomatic codes being used by the various legations in Rome prior to World War II, giving *il Duce* an unparalleled fund of secret knowledge. In August 1941, the SIM burgled the code safe of the American military attaché in Rome, Colonel Norman E. Fiske, with the help of one Loris Gherardi, an Italian employed as a messenger by the American Embassy. What the SIM got was the U.S. "Black Code" (so-called because of the color of its binding), used for all U.S. diplomatic and diplomatic-military communications. The SIM shared this treasure with the Abwehr, after which the European Axis had nearly complete access to U.S. diplomatic communications. The most important use to which they put the stolen code was in reading the messages transmitted by the American military attaché in Cairo, Colonel Bonner Frank Fellers.

In 1941 and 1942, Colonel Bonner F. Fellers (seen here later in the war, when he was Douglas MacArthur's Assistant Chief of Staff) was the U.S. military attaché in Cairo. His detailed reports on the British military situation were intercepted and decrypted by Italian Military Intelligence.

Over the winter of 1941 to 1942, as the Axis forces were building up for their spring offensive, Fellers reported on the strength and disposition of British units and provided important elements of Auchinleck's defensive plans. His most dramatic report included the details of a plan to fight a convoy through to Malta, relieving the island and rejuvenating its ability to attack Axis supply convoys. Fellers reported on the plans for a series of commando raids designed to take out the bomber bases from which the Regia Aeronautica and the Luftwaffe would attack the convoy. Thus forewarned, the Germans took precautions and repulsed the commandos, inflicting heavy casualties.

In July 1942, a German prisoner of war hinted to the British that Fellers' signals were being read in Deutsches Afrika Korps headquarters. The British themselves began to listen in (having broken the Black Code some years before) and informed the American authorities. Fellers was not told what had happened, but was immediately recalled to Washington.

In part because of the growing importance of American military aid to the British war effort, Fellers was closely tied into the deliberations of the British High Command in North Africa. He extensively toured the fronts (the B-dienst praised his energy), reporting on British morale, on how the British army used lend-lease equipment, on tactics, problems, and progress made by British forces on the battlefront. All this was faithfully relayed via wireless to the U.S. Military Intelligence Division in Washington (MILID WASH).

Axis radio monitoring stations listened in and reported every word to Rommel, often within hours of transmission—and often before it was even read in Washington.

His replacement brought with him a new military cipher, which the Axis (and possibly even the British) found impenetrable. Rommel thus was cut off from his source just as the Desert War reached its crisis point.

Fellers' security had been checked and found faultless. There was, of course, no way that he could have known that his reports were being read by the enemy: in making them, he was simply doing his job as military attaché. Nevertheless, in reading the transmissions, the British found that he had been critical of their conduct of the war and pessimistic about their chances. And so Fellers became *persona non grata* in Cairo, though he later became a brigadier general on MacArthur's staff.

ABOVE: Rommel, seen here with binoculars and his trademark goggles. The German commander's uncanny ability to make the most of his limited forces and hold the much larger Allied armies at bay owed much to superior German capabilities in tactical military intelligence.

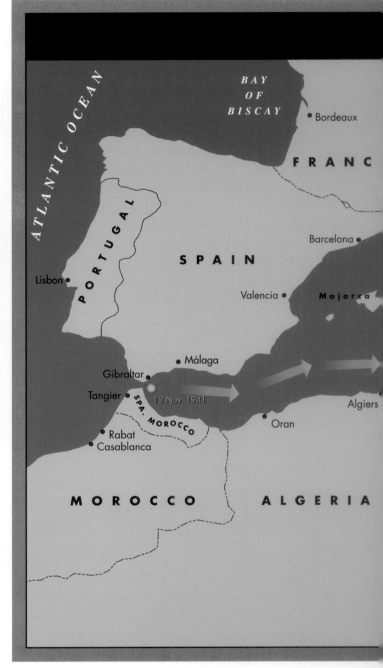

Achilles' heel: the supply lines stretching across the Mediterranean from Italy to Tripoli.

The key to the Mediterranean was the island of Malta, located on a direct line between Sicily and the main Italian port in North Africa, Tripoli. The British had held Malta for more than a century, and as long as they did so, they had a base from which to strike with aircraft,

# The Mediterranean: 1940–1941

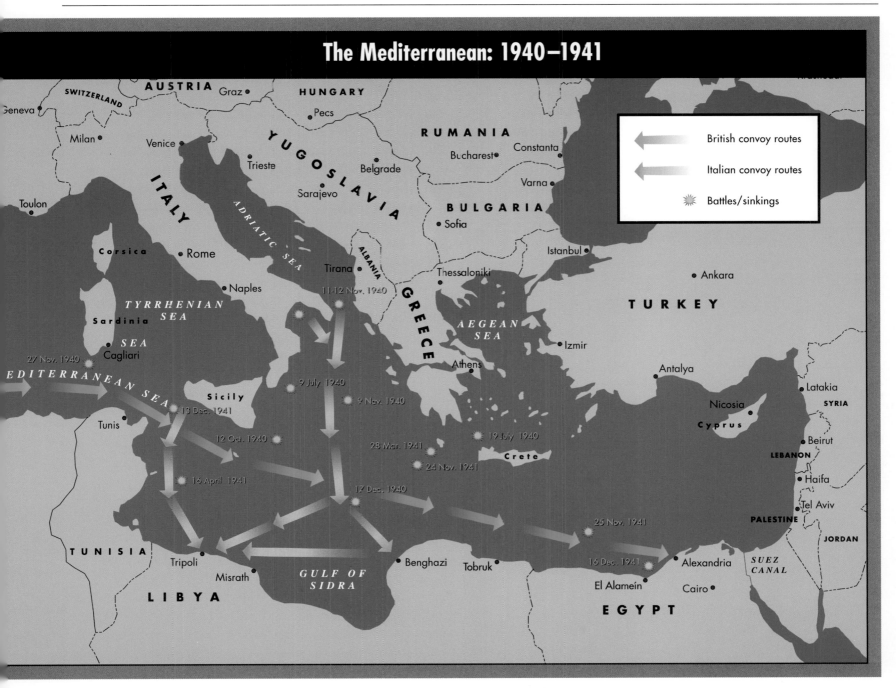

*British convoy routes*

*Italian convoy routes*

*Battles/sinkings*

surface ships, and submarines at the Axis convoys carrying supplies and reinforcements to North Africa. Using ULTRA to locate and identify the convoys, the British decimated Rommel's supplies over the fall and winter of 1941. Sensitive to the importance of keeping the ULTRA secret, the British were careful to send out reconnaissance planes to "find" a convoy once it had been

ABOVE: Axis supply convoys coming from Taranto, Bari, or Naples had to swing wide to avoid the Allied air and naval forces based on Malta. Using ULTRA, the British were nonetheless able to locate and attack the supply convoys. Supplies that made it through were unloaded at Tripoli or (less often) Benghazi. Both ports were miles behind the front lines, especially as Rommel began his advance into Egypt. Ironically, the more successful Rommel was in his war against the British, the less secure his supplies became. By the time he reached El Alamein, near Alexandria, his army was worn out and desperately short of food, water, and fuel. Most Allied supply convoys took the much longer, but safer, route around Africa, north into the Red Sea and finally through the Suez Canal. Those that did risk the journey through the Mediterranean were subjected to constant Axis air and naval attack.

# ULTRA and the Hecatomb of Tankers

For the Regia Marina, the great trauma of World War II was the struggle to maintain the Axis supply lines to North Africa. In this ongoing battle, the Italians lost more than two million tons of shipping: nearly all their merchant marine, not to mention heavy losses in warships and crews. Unbeknownst to the Italians until long after World War II, most of these losses could be directly attributed to ULTRA.

When Italy entered the war, the Regia Marina used an effective hand-cipher system that remained impervious to attack by the British cryptanalysts at Bletchley Park. Italian naval communications thus remained secure until the Italian high command yielded to pressure from the Germans to adopt a version of the ENIGMA machine. Ironically, the Germans, whose own ciphers were rapidly becoming transparent, were worried about the security of the Italian ciphers, which the British could not read.

Early in 1941, Supermarina adopted a Swedish-built version of the ENIGMA machine, the C38, which in Italian service became the C38m.

Sunken Italian merchant ships in Naples harbor. Italian use of ENIGMA—adopted at the insistence of the Germans—made their communications transparent to Allied cryptanalysts. Most Italian merchantmen were sunk at sea, but Allied strategic bombers struck them wherever they could be found.

Bletchley Park broke into the new Italian cipher by the summer of 1941. Soon, British cryptanalysts were reading Italian signals with a regularity that exceeded even their ability to read German ciphers.

The most important use of this new source of signals intelligence was in attacking the convoy routes that connected Axis troops in North Africa with their Italian sources of supply. The ULTRA that was being received from the Italian ciphers gave dates of departure from Italy and arrival in North Africa, route, speed, cargoes, and even the names of the ships being sent. All the British had to do was to plot an intercept course and be in the right place at the right time. To guard the ULTRA secret, they made sure that Italian convoys were "discovered" by search aircraft or some other form of reconnaissance before they were attacked.

In October 1941, the British Admiralty dispatched a force of light cruisers and destroyers ("Force K") to their base at Malta, astride the Italian convoy routes to North Africa. Force K joined aircraft and subs already based there in attacks on Italian merchant shipping. Operating at night, using radar (which the Italians did not yet have), they devastated the Italian convoy routes. Whole convoys were wiped out. The Italian destroyer escorts resisted bravely, but generally were overwhelmed by the superior, radar-equipped British force. The Regia Marina's casualties were terrible. The British naval offensive was timed to coincide with Operation Crusader, the attack into Axis-held Cyrenaica, and with good effect. Rommel's efforts to stave off the British attacks were crippled by lack of fuel and supplies. Finally, Supermarina resorted to powerful escorts of battleships and heavy cruisers, a drastic measure that consumed far more materiel than was actually being delivered to North African ports, but by December the convoys were getting through. At about the same time, Force K was almost wiped out when it ran into an uncharted minefield. Over the following spring, a concerted air and naval offensive against Malta eased the supply situation.

But with the British offensive out of El Alamein, the Royal Navy again was on the attack in the Central Mediterranean. Using ULTRA decrypts of Italian C38m signals, they were even able to single out specific types of ships (primarily tankers) for attack. Chronically short of fuel, the Regia Marina could do little to protect the ships daily sailing with fuel and war materials. In this period, known to the Italian navy as the "hecatomb of tankers," the Italian merchant marine lost 972 ships, of some 1,300,000 tons—more than double their losses of the previous two years.

In a scene reminiscent of the Battle of Britain, British pilots based in Cyprus run to their Hurricanes. Air power was key to controlling the Mediterranean, but the Allied victory owed as much to the ULTRA secret as to anything else.

located by signals intelligence. British intelligence had not been able to read Italian signals until the Germans insisted that Italian wireless procedures be brought into line with German practice. Supermarina thus adopted a version of the ENIGMA machine that was read with relative ease by the code-breakers in Bletchley Park.

Supermarina and the German naval high command recognized the importance of eliminating Malta and urged a combined airborne and amphibious assault on the island, but Rommel refused to be diverted from his goal of conquering Cairo. Instead, the Luftwaffe and the Italian Air Force (*Regia Aeronautica*) pummeled Malta with bombs.

Finally, Auchinleck was ready to begin his assault. Operation Crusader was launched on November 18, 1941, with two reinforced corps. The British had a distinct numerical superiority in tanks and aircraft. Rommel was short of supplies and perilously low on fuel. Moreover, the Auk knew from ULTRA that Rommel had pulled many of his troops out of line for another

assault on Tobruk. He struck deep across the border from Egypt, knowing that he was attacking Rommel's rear flank. In a series of swirling battles in November and December 1941, Rommel inflicted heavy casualties on the British, but, due to the lack of fuel, was finally compelled to withdraw from Cyrenaica back to El Agheila, where he had begun. Reinforced by supplies and fuel from the Italian "battleship convoys," Rommel counterattacked on January 5, 1942, retaking part of Cyrenaica.

Auchinleck planned an amphibious assault for June 1942 against Rommel's rear (Acrobat), but was warned by ULTRA of an Axis plan to take Tobruk and strike out for Cairo. He dug in with the Eighth Army west of Tobruk, at Gazala. But Rommel's battlefield intelligence served him well yet again: outflanking the British position and surrounding much of Auchinleck's armor, the Axis forces took Tobruk on June 21, 1942, and forced the British to retreat. From Italian intercepts of Colonel Fellers' transmissions from Cairo, Rommel knew that the British position in North Africa was

Italian general staff officers contemplate a difficult war. Most Axis troops in North Africa were Italian. Although Rommel held his allies in barely concealed contempt, his Italian troops fought bravely for him, despite being poorly equipped and often badly led. The Italian navy suffered heavy casualties in its heroic efforts to keep the Axis armies in North Africa supplied. Italian military intelligence scored the Axis intelligence coup of the war when it stole the American Black Code and brought Rommel priceless intelligence on British strengths and dispositions at the height of the North African campaign.

crumbling and he drove relentlessly on to Cairo. Auchinleck conducted a masterful retreat and finally halted Rommel's advance at El Alamein, a small railway station just west of Cairo. Over the summer of 1942, Auchinleck was replaced as commander of the Eighth Army by Sir Bernard Law Montgomery.

Rommel was now in real trouble. His supply lines stretched all the way back to Tripoli, his tanks were worn out, and his men were exhausted. These had been problems before, but he had been able to compensate by a superior knowledge of the battlefield. Now, however, his tactical reconnaissance units were gone, decimated in the fighting around Gazala. In Cairo, Fellers had been replaced, and the Military Attaché's office in Cairo began using wartime U.S. codes, so that source was gone, too. Meanwhile, although the Regia Marina, the Regia Aeronautica, and the Luftwaffe had been able to

isolate Malta, the RAF was decimating his supply lines on land. Using ULTRA to identify when shipments were leaving Tripoli by truck, RAF fighter-bombers and bombers caught them in the desert and destroyed them before they could reach the Axis' front lines. The Axis forces in Africa had enough strength left for one more attack, which they mounted in August, against the British position on the ridge at Alam Halfa. Rommel did everything he could to deceive the British about his intentions, but ULTRA intercepts gave away the whole German plan of attack. The German offensive collapsed and the Axis forces dug in to await the inevitable British assault.

"Monty" was more careful than any previous Allied commander in the desert. Using ULTRA, he identified the Italian units in Rommel's army and planned a massive attack designed to single them out in the hopes that the

Italians would break quickly and retreat, leaving the German forces stranded. In fact, when the attack came late in October 1942, it worked the other way around: the Germans took all the available transport and left the Italians to hold off the British. The Italian units fought tenaciously before being overwhelmed by superior British forces. Far to the west, American troops landed on the coasts of Algeria and French Morocco on November 8, 1942 (Operation Torch). Rommel was driven in retreat all the way to Tunis. On January 23, 1943, Montgomery and the Eighth Army entered Tripoli.

Although Allied commanders continued to rely on ULTRA and other sources for valuable intelligence about the Axis, after the Torch landings, the Allied superiority in men and materiel rapidly outstripped intelligence in importance to the Anglo-American war effort in North Africa and the Mediterranean. Rommel still had a few surprises left in him, as he demonstrated in his defeat of the U.S. Second Corps at the Battle of Kasserine Pass, an Allied intelligence failure of the first order. But so great was Allied superiority that such victories were in the long run immaterial.

Italian soldiers man a 75mm gun battery in North Africa.

# Chapter 6

# Signals Intelligence and the Battle of the Atlantic

THE BATTLE OF THE ATLANTIC WAS THE NAME GIVEN TO THE GERMAN attempt to defeat Great Britain by disrupting the overseas transport of supplies upon which she depended for her very existence. Maintenance of these lines of supply was vital to the Allied war effort: without victory in the Battle of the Atlantic, the strategic bombing offensive and the Allied invasion of France would not have been possible.

Both the British and German naval high commands began the war with fundamental misconceptions of how this battle would be fought and won. The British believed that the development of sonar (which they then referred to as ASDIC) had effectively neutralized German U-boats as a danger to Allied shipping. Using sonar, escorted convoys and ASDIC-equipped destroyers would keep German surface raiders and U-boats alike at bay, preventing a repetition of the shipping crises of World War I, when Britain had been close to starvation.

In the eyes of the commander-in-chief of the Kriegsmarine, Grand Admiral Erich Raeder, and SKL (*die Seekriegsleitung*), the German

The German *Panzerschiff* (armored ship) *Deutschland* was the first of a class of three powerful warships, also known as "pocket battleships," built especially for commerce warfare.

Grossadmiral Erich Raeder (third from right), Commander in Chief of the German navy from 1928 to 1943, inspects a newly built U-boat. Raeder built a small but balanced fleet to prey on British shipping. A key element in German strategy was the Funk-Beobachtungsdienst, or B-Dienst, the signals intelligence unit of the small German navy, which used intercepted signals to track British naval dispositions, thereby offsetting Allied numerical superiority. In German plans, U-boats were to be used alongside surface ships and aircraft in coordinated attacks. The small size of the German fleet at the outbreak of war made it less effective than Raeder had hoped, but the Kriegsmarine's real Achilles' heel was its heavy reliance on the ENIGMA machine for its wireless communications. British success in decrypting German naval communications overshadowed German successes. Ironically, for a period in 1942, each side was reading the other's communications— and neither was aware that the other was doing it.

Naval War Staff, World War I had taught that U-boats alone would not be sufficient to cut the transoceanic supply lines upon which Great Britain depended for food and supplies of every kind. So instead they planned a combined assault, using aircraft, surface ships, and U-boats in coordinated attacks. A key element of the German strategy—eventually to predominate in the Battle of the Atlantic—was the use of "Wolfpacks" of U-boats in night surface attacks. This effectively neutralized the British use of ASDIC and presented the British with tactical problems in the war at sea that were insoluble until large numbers of antisubmarine aircraft and surface escorts equipped with radar became available.

Essential to both sides was the use of wireless communications. All navies used wireless to control and coordinate the movements of their own warships and to locate targets by monitoring the signals of their opponents. The Wolfpack tactics of the Flag Officer, U-boats, Vice Admiral Karl Dönitz, in particular, depended on the heavy use of wireless to coordinate convoy attacks: U-boats in patrol lines would be spread across the shipping routes, lying in wait for convoys. The first U-boat to sight a convoy would not attack, but serve as contact holder, relaying its position to U-boat headquarters (initially in Berlin, later in Lorient and Paris). There, Dönitz and his staff would use wireless to assemble the available U-boats in a coordinated attack, usually at night.

The Germans relied on the use of their ENIGMA cipher machines to keep their communications secure. Even though the Kriegsmarine eventually used a more complex version, with four rotors instead of the usual three, and practiced much better wireless discipline than either the Luftwaffe or the army, the heavy use of wireless in *Rudeltaktik* (Wolfpack tactics) left their signals vulnerable to British attack. Even so, Bletchley Park was unable to penetrate German naval signals in a timely fashion until mid-1941. Thereafter, they acquired a steadily increasing knowledge of German codes until they were able to read most of the Kriegsmarine's operational communications. Until that time, the Royal Navy's Operational Intelligence Centre (OIC) made extensive use of traffic analysis and radio direction finding (RDF) in its efforts to monitor the movements of German naval units.

The Kriegsmarine, by contrast, began the war with a good knowledge of British codes and communications. The Royal Navy had broken out its wartime codes in the Ethiopian crisis of 1935 for its operations in the Mediterranean. These had been monitored by the Italian SIS, who had shared their breakthrough with their allies. Units of the *Funk-Beobachtungsdienst*, or *B-dienst*, the Kriegsmarine's radio intercept service, were posted on board every major German warship, to supplement the activities of the main installation in Berlin.

The Kriegsmarine never achieved the level of success in signals intelligence that the British did, but they were able to track British naval movements with a high degree of confidence from the beginning of the war, a mastery of British communications they maintained in general until a complete change in British codes and ciphers took place in 1943. This meant that each side was reading the other's signals from the last half of 1941 through all of 1942. Despite this, neither side ever stumbled onto the other's success in deciphering signals intelligence until later.

In August 1939, the German navy had sent two pocket battleships (*Deutschland* and *Admiral Graf Spee*) out to waiting positions in the North and South Atlantic. The available U-boats took up positions off the British

A merchant ship burns after being torpedoed by a U-boat. The German naval high command relied heavily on communications to coordinate attacks on Allied convoys in the Atlantic. When British intelligence broke the ENIGMA codes, they were able to intercept and read these communications. Using this information to plot the U-boats' locations, the British Admiralty in London could divert convoys away from the Germans and send in destroyers and aircraft to seek out and sink the U-boats lying in wait.

coasts. Apart from some light cruisers and a few destroyers, no other German warships were ready for action at
the outbreak of war. Although German reporting on
British fleet dispositions was fairly accurate, the Germans
were not able to make much use of it when war broke
out in September. Dönitz did try to use signals intelligence to track down the aircraft carrier *Courageous*, but
unsuccessfully. The aircraft carrier was sunk anyway,
but by another U-boat, one not involved in the chase.
Two battleships, *Scharnhorst* and *Gneisenau*, became
available in October, as did the heavy cruiser *Admiral
Hipper*, and SKL used them in two sorties into the North
Atlantic to tie up British capital ships in home waters,
preventing them from being used to hunt down the two
pocket battleships. The B-dienst was able to plot British
warship movements pretty consistently during this period, but was unable to prevent the *Admiral Graf Spee*
from being hunted down and trapped in the neutral port
of Montevideo, Uruguay, where she was scuttled.

The next April, Germany occupied Denmark and
Norway, a move that was considerably eased by the
British inability to read the Kriegsmarine's ENIGMA.
Bletchley Park detected the movement of naval units
prior to the invasion, but thought it presaged a breakout
into the Atlantic. Thus, even though the Allies themselves were preparing a move into Norwegian waters,
they were unable to act quickly enough to prevent the
occupation. Although French and British troops occupied Narvik and Trondheim, they had to withdraw the
following June to meet the German invasion of France.

B-dienst intercepts of the communications surrounding the evacuation brought the German battleships
*Scharnhorst* and *Gneisenau* out of port, along with the
heavy cruiser *Admiral Hipper* (Operation Juno). Together,
these ships sank several transports, but the real prize
came when *Scharnhorst* and *Gneisenau* caught and sank
the British aircraft carrier *Glorious*, sister ship of the
*Courageous* (although both German battleships were
heavily damaged in the engagement and out of commission until the end of the year).

The fall of France in the summer of 1940, which
gave the Kriegsmarine access to ports on the English
Channel and the Bay of Biscay, was the beginning of
what German U-boat men later called the "Happy

OPPOSITE: Adolf Hitler and
Erich Raeder attend the launch
of the battleship *Scharnhorst*
in 1936. The Germans built
powerful battleships such as
the *Scharnhorst* and her sister
ship, the *Gneisenau*, to
function as commerce raiders.

The brunt of the German U-boat campaign was borne by Type VII C U-boats such as this one. German U-boats scored their most noteworthy success during the first "Happy Time," over the summer and early fall of 1940. Operating from newly won French bases on the Bay of Biscay, the U-boats used intelligence to locate and attack the British convoys bringing vital supplies into British ports. Fortunately for the British, there never were enough U-boats available to inflict a decisive defeat. By the time more U-boats became available, the British had more and better anti-submarine escorts, and the priceless advantage of ULTRA.

Time." Within days of the French surrender, Dönitz had dispatched trains loaded with spare parts and torpedoes to set up bases at the French naval ports of Brest, Lorient, St. Nazaire, and La Pallice. All these ports were close to the British North Atlantic convoy routes, which allowed U-boats to spend much more time on station than when they had been operating out of Germany and brought Dönitz's system of centrally controlled Wolfpacks to its full potential.

There are many reasons for the disastrous losses suffered by the British over the fall, winter, and spring of 1940 to 1941, including inadequate numbers of convoy escorts, lack of radar and the tactics to defeat the German night surface attacks, and a near total absence of aircraft capable of operating over the central ocean. But foremost among them was the work done by the German B-dienst in plotting the British convoy routes and vectoring the U-boats into attack, principally through traffic analysis and radio direction finding.

It was fortunate for the Allied cause that Dönitz never had sufficient numbers of U-boats during this period to severely cripple the British war effort. Even so, during the first Happy Time (June to October 1940), a very small number of U-boats (no more than eleven to thirteen were generally available) sank a total of

1,395,298 tons of British and Allied shipping, an average of 279,060 tons per month. Sinkings fell off slightly thereafter, due to the onset of winter weather, a gradual increase in the numbers of British convoy escorts available, and improved antisubmarine warfare (ASW) tactics. From October 1940 on, however, the U-boats were aided by the presence of German surface ships on the high seas, which caused the British to disperse convoys and divert their escorts to other tasks, so that, even in the winter, sinkings averaged 264,723 tons per month.

The first German heavy ship to sortie was the pocket battleship *Admiral Scheer*, which began a highly successful five-month cruise in October 1940. Next to enter the North Atlantic was the heavy cruiser *Admiral Hipper*, which carried out two cruises, one in December 1940, the other in February 1941, after a four-week refit in Brest.

The high point of German surface force operations in the Atlantic came between January and June 1941, beginning with the three-month cruise of the battleships *Scharnhorst* and *Gneisenau* over January, February, and March 1941. In May, the new battleship *Bismarck* put to sea with the heavy cruiser *Prinz Eugen*. *Bismarck* sank the powerful British battle cruiser *Hood*, but later was hunted down and sunk by the British Home Fleet. The German commander, Admiral Günther Lütjens, had incorrectly believed that he was being shadowed by cruisers. He thus made free use of his wireless, in the belief (which at the time was correct) that his signals could not be read. His excessive use of wireless gave away his position. *Bismarck*'s consort, *Prinz Eugen*, put into Brest, where she joined *Scharnhorst* and *Gneisenau*, which had been there since March. A further sortie by the pocket battleship *Lützow* (the renamed *Deutschland*) was aborted in June when she was torpedoed by British torpedo bombers off the Norwegian coast. The Germans attempted no further sorties with their surface warships, largely because they were all being either refitted or repaired as a result of damage suffered during RAF bomber attacks, which were inflicting significant losses during this period.

In the winter of 1941 to 1942, Hitler ordered the German heavy ships in Brest to redeploy up the English

LEFT: Torpedoed by a U-boat, a tanker sinks in the North Atlantic. The Battle of the Atlantic was a grim struggle, with quarter neither sought nor given by either side. The crews of tankers like this one were often incinerated with their ships. Merchant seamen who survived a sinking frequently drowned or died of exposure in open boats. The crews of depth-charged U-boats usually died horribly when the submarines plunged to the bottom and imploded.
LEFT BELOW: The launch of the battleship *Bismarck*. Sunk after a chase that extended from the Skagerrak to the coast of France, the *Bismarck* was betrayed by her commander's excessive use of wireless. Although the British could not yet read German naval codes when the *Bismarck* was sunk, they were able to identify the pattern of her transmissions and home in on her position.

RIGHT: The battleship *Gneisenau* moored in Brest after a three-month cruise during which she and her sister ship, the *Scharnhorst*, sunk 22 British and Allied merchant ships. As flagship, the *Gneisenau* had a B-Dienst team on board that provided the Fleet Commander, Admiral Günther Lütjens, with up-to-the-minute signals intelligence. In February 1942, the *Gneisenau* escaped back to Germany through the English Channel (in a maneuver now known as the "Channel Dash"), but was crippled in a British air raid while in port and never put to sea again. BELOW RIGHT: The battleship *Tirpitz* under air attack in a Norwegian fjord. Sister ship to the *Bismarck*, the *Tirpitz* never saw combat against the Royal Navy, but was the focal point of British naval strategy in European waters until she was sunk by high-level bombers late in 1944. OPPOSITE: The German heavy cruiser *Prinz Eugen*, seen here during the Channel Dash, survived the *Bismarck* operation but fell victim to ULTRA when she sailed for Norway in March 1942. Using signals intelligence to plot her course, the Admiralty sent in the submarine *Trident*, which torpedoed the *Prinz Eugen*, causing such heavy damage that she had to return to Germany for repairs.

Channel to Norway, where he thought they would be put to better use attacking the Arctic convoys carrying supplies to the Soviet Union—and because he feared a British attack there. SKL bitterly fought this, but eventually gave way. Operation Cerberus (the so-called "Channel Dash") was a tactical success in that all the ships arrived home—albeit with some damage—but it prevented the Kriegsmarine's surface ships from carrying out their intended role in the Battle of the Atlantic. Over the course of 1942, most of the German surface fleet was redeployed to Norway, where it operated against the British convoys bound for the Soviet Arctic port of Murmansk with some success, most notably in the destruction of convoy PQ 17 (see page 98–99). But they were increasingly immobilized by a lack of fuel and hamstrung by restrictions Hitler imposed upon their use.

Unbeknownst to the Germans, however, the real reason behind the loss of the *Bismarck* and the torpedoing of the *Lützow* was British use of signals intelligence in the war at sea. Since the beginning of the war, the British Admiralty's Operational Intelligence Centre (OIC) had been studying German naval operations. OIC was initially unable to read German naval ENIGMA signals, but it had access to Luftwaffe ENIGMA (which often provided insights into naval operations) and made good use of radio direction finding and traffic analysis, as well as prisoner of war interrogations and other sources of information. By May 1941, OIC officials were experienced enough at this that they were able to track down the *Bismarck* by identifying the unique character of her wireless signals and plotting her course using RDF.

Then, in May 1941 (too late for the *Bismarck* operation) Bletchley Park mastered both the general ciphers used by German warships in home waters and the operational codes used by U-boats on the high seas. The first fruit of this breakthrough was the torpedoing of the *Lützow*, whose sortie was detected through ENIGMA. The following month, the British used ENIGMA decrypts to locate the eight supply ships that had put to sea to support the cruise of the *Bismarck* and the *Prinz Eugen*. This was the cause of much worrying at OIC, for it was feared that the sudden destruction of so many ships in such a short period of time would alert the Germans to

# Signals Intelligence and the Sinking of the *Atlantis*

In addition to regular warships, the Germans made use of converted merchant ships known as *Hilfskreuzern*, or auxiliary cruisers, in their war on British overseas trade. The auxiliary cruisers were given armament of 6-inch (15cm) guns and, disguised as Allied ships or neutrals, sent out to prey on Allied shipping. Although the losses they inflicted were pinpricks compared to those imposed by the U-boats, they were quite successful in tying down Allied warships searching for them and delaying and diverting Allied merchant traffic. The most successful raider, Ship 16 *Atlantis*, was at sea for more than a year and sank twenty-two Allied merchant ships of 145,697 tons. A contributing factor to their success was that Bletchley Park never successfully penetrated the cipher they used. When these auxiliary cruisers were located, it was mostly by chance, or when their mission brought them into contact with the U-boats.

Which is what happened to *Atlantis*. In November 1941, she was ordered to rendezvous with and refuel *U-126* in the South Atlantic, just south of the equator. SKL's instructions to *Atlantis* could not be read, but those sent to *U-126* were. When *Atlantis* rendezvoused with *U-126* on November 22, the big, fast, heavy cruiser *Devonshire* was waiting in the area. After a brief reconnaissance, she moved in and sank *Atlantis* in a matter of minutes. Knowing there was at least one U-boat in the area, she quickly moved off, picking up no survivors.

*U-126* surfaced and organized *Atlantis*' ship's boats and flotsam into a small convoy of rafts with her captain, Bernhard Rogge, and about 100 survivors on board. They next rendezvoused with the U-boat supply ship *Python*. However, once again, the necessary communications betrayed them. The *Python* was intercepted by the British heavy cruiser *Dorsetshire*. Being unarmed, the German ship scuttled herself. The two U-boats in the vicinity submerged. Once again, the British ship moved off. There were now about 414 survivors from both German surface ships. Other U-boats, including some Italian boats, were vectored in to assist with rescue attempts. After an epic journey of some 5,000 miles (8,045km), all the survivors were dropped off in France.

The British County-class cruiser *Dorsetshire* (seen here in 1929 ) sank the U-boat supply ship *Python* with survivors from the German raider *Atlantis* on board. Her sister ship, the *Devonshire*, was responsible for sinking the *Atlantis*. In both instances, the British cruisers were alerted to the presence of the German ships by the Admiralty, using ULTRA intercepts. OPPOSITE: A German seaman in the water. Survivors from the disguised raider *Atlantis* barely made it home after their ship was sunk by a British heavy cruiser. ULTRA contributed to the sinking of their ship, and hindered the rescue efforts mounted by the Kriegsmarine.

the fact that their ciphers had been compromised. As it happened, however, many of the ships were located by other means, so the secret was safe.

Over the next six months, the Battle of the Atlantic assumed the character of a duel between OIC and Dönitz's U-boat High Command. Using ENIGMA decrypts, OIC rerouted convoys to avoid German attacks and reinforce the escort groups of those threatened. Losses in the Atlantic plummeted from a high of nearly 326,000 tons in May 1941 to a low of just over 56,000 tons in November (though September and October had been bad months, both with losses approaching 200,000 tons. Although U-boat losses remained low at first, as they had been throughout most of the war thus far, ten boats were lost in December. The sudden reversals in fortune made Dönitz and his staff suspicious, but they never suspected a compromise of the supposedly impenetrable ENIGMA cipher.

Then, in January 1942, the entry of the United States into the war created a bountiful new hunting ground for the U-boats off the East Coast of the United States. The primitive antisubmarine measures then in use by the U.S. Navy were easily circumvented by the experienced German U-boat commanders, and Allied shipping losses once again began to rise. In

OPPOSITE: The *Panzerschiff Lützow* (formerly the *Deutschland*), seen here in a prewar photograph, sortied for an Atlantic raiding cruise a few weeks after the *Bismarck* was sunk. But the British were warned of the sortie by ULTRA. Torpedo bombers caught and damaged the *Lützow* off the Norwegian coast, inflicting sufficient damage to force her to turn back. ABOVE: The *Bismarck*, seen here firing on the British battle cruiser *Hood*, was the last German battleship to enter the Atlantic on a war cruise.

# The Destruction of Convoy PQ 17

When Hitler attacked the Soviet Union in June 1941, Great Britain's immediate response was to begin sending military supplies and aid via the Arctic port of Murmansk, situated on the Kola Peninsula. The route was a dangerous one, extending all along the coast of German-occupied Norway into the Barents Sea, around North Cape, and into Murmansk. The first convoys proceeded relatively unopposed, but, over the winter of 1941 to 1942, the Germans began a buildup of naval forces in Trondheim and in the fjords around North Cape. In February 1942, the battleship *Tirpitz*, sister ship to the *Bismarck*, moved north.

The buildup continued over the following spring, hindered by the constant threat of air attack and by a chronic shortage of fuel. It was monitored closely by OIC and Bletchley Park—all communications associated with German naval movements being sent in home waters via ENIGMA, which the British had been reading since May 1941. Nevertheless, by June 1942, the Germans had assembled a force of one battleship (*Tirpitz*), two pocket battleships (*Lützow* and *Admiral Scheer*), one heavy cruiser (*Admiral Hipper*), and eight destroyers, along with U-boats and Luftwaffe bomber units specially trained for attacks on shipping.

To counter this formidable collection of naval forces the next convoy to Murmansk was to be heavily escorted. With the convoy itself was a strong force of destroyers and escort vessels. "Close escort" was provided by a force of four heavy cruisers under Rear Admiral L.H.K. Hamilton. "Distant escort" consisted of two battleships (HMS *Duke of York* and the American USS *Washington*), an aircraft carrier (HMS *Victorious*), and two cruisers and destroyers, under the Commander, Home Fleet, Admiral Sir John Tovey. However, because of the heavy Luftwaffe concentration in northern Norway, the battleships would not proceed into the Barents Sea (in effect, they would abandon the convoy precisely at the most dangerous point of attack). This left a convoy escort consisting entirely of destroyers and cruisers—adequate in the face of aircraft, U-boat, or cruiser attack, but quite unable to take on the *Tirpitz*.

The German plan of attack, Operation Rösselsprung ("Knight's-Move"), was put into action when the convoy set sail on June 27, 1942. In the Admiralty, the OIC and the British commander-in-chief, First Sea Lord Admiral Sir Dudley Pound, watched the German preparations with growing unease via the Kriegsmarine's ENIGMA traffic. Pound had to decide what to do should the *Tirpitz* sortie. If this were to happen after Tovey and his battleships had turned back, there would be no alternative but to scatter the convoy and withdraw the escorts. The merchant ships would be left on their own to await destruction.

In July 1942, Convoy PQ 17, seen here in the Barents Sea, in a photograph taken from a German reconnaissance aircraft, was dispersed by the Admiralty, to prevent it from being attacked by the German battleship *Tirpitz*. Merchant ships were safest from submarine or air attack while in convoy. A convoy was "dispersed," or broken up, only if a surface ship threatened—spreading the ships out made them harder for a surface warship to find. But such tactics left the merchantmen horribly vulnerable to air and submarine attack.

Early on July 4, Tovey and his battleship and aircraft carrier force turned back, according to plan. That evening, the Admiralty received an ULTRA intercept from the German Fleet commander, Admiral Otto Schniewind, showing that the *Tirpitz* was arriving in Altenfjord, near North Cape, with destroyers, and ordering preparation to refuel his ships for the planned attack.

Pound wrongly interpreted this to mean that the *Tirpitz* was about to put to sea against the convoy. In fact, as OIC was aware, the signal meant only that preparations were under way: Schniewind would not take his ships to sea until he had received confirmation of his orders from the High Command, which would be apparent in German wireless traffic. Pound did not consult the OIC, however, but sent the following signal on July 4 at 2100 hours:

CRUISER FORCE TO WITHDRAW TO WESTWARD AT
HIGH SPEED.

Another signal was sent to the convoy a few minutes later:

IMMEDIATE. OWING TO THREAT FROM SURFACE
SHIPS CONVOY IS TO DISPERSE AND TO PROCEED
TO RUSSIAN PORTS.

The German force actually did put to sea the following day, but was recalled after only a brief sortie. With the escorts gone, the surface ships were hardly needed. One by one, bombers and U-boats hunted down the hapless merchant ships. Of the thirty-five ships that had sailed with convoy PQ 17, only eleven reached Murmansk.

The battleship *Tirpitz*, by its mere presence, had destroyed a convoy; ironically, without the great secret, ULTRA, it would never have happened.

ABOVE RIGHT: German submarines and land-based bombers wreaked havoc among the dispersed ships of convoy PQ 17, sinking 24 of 35 merchants ships bound for the Soviet port of Murmansk. Here, a German U-boat torpedoes a freighter from the convoy. RIGHT: Crewmen of the German *U-703* are decorated after the action at the base of the 11th U-boat Flotilla in Bergen, Norway. Their commander, Kapitanleutnant Heinz Bielfeld (left) looks on.

February, the Kriegsmarine introduced a new version of the ENIGMA machine with four rotors, and Bletchley Park lost all ability to read the U-boats' operational signals. The first six months of 1942 were, in consequence, known as the second "Happy Time": shipping losses averaged more than 500,000 tons per month, with U-boat losses once again relatively low. After June 1942, improved ASW tactics and weapons, including more and better aircraft (both long-range, land-based bombers and new ASW escort carriers) brought U-boat losses up again, but 1942 was still their most successful year: altogether, U-boats sank more than 6 million tons of Allied shipping.

The crisis point of the U-boat war was reached in the first half of 1943. The number of operational U-boats had steadily increased in 1941 and 1942, so that by January 1943 more than 400 were available, of which about 100 were at sea at any given time. By March, an unendurable average of 22 percent of the Allied merchant ships at sea every month was being sunk. U-boat losses were also high, mainly due to the vastly increased and improved number of aircraft and escorts available to the Allies. Then in May 1943, Bletchley Park finally penetrated the new four-rotor ENIGMA cipher.

In fact, the German navy probably was already losing this battle of attrition, but Bletchley Park's breakthrough broke the back of the U-boat offensive once and for all. In May 1943 alone, forty-seven U-boats were sunk in the North Atlantic. From that point on, U-boat losses increased dramatically and Allied shipping losses plummeted. The Battle of the Atlantic had been won. Although it may safely be said that it would been won without ULTRA, it has been estimated that breaking the German ENIGMA ciphers shortened the war by at least a year.

Maneuvering at high speed, a British destroyer hauls around to attack a submerged U-boat. Although intelligence contributed greatly to the Allied victory in the Battle of the Atlantic, in the final analysis it was escorts such as this one, present in ever growing numbers, that defeated the German U-boat offensive.

An American destroyer escort drops depth charges on a submerged U-boat. The German U-boat service suffered 80 percent casualties in the course of World War II, with most of their losses incurred in attacks such as these.

# Chapter 7

# Intelligence and the Victory in Europe

MEETING JUST OUTSIDE CASABLANCA, MOROCCO, IN JANUARY 1943, BRITISH Prime Minister Winston Churchill, U.S. President Franklin D. Roosevelt, and the military and political leaders of Great Britain and the United States decided upon what effectively would be the strategy for the defeat of Germany. In broad terms, the plan was to destroy German war potential in a combined strategic bombing offensive, while gearing up in Great Britain for an invasion of the Continent, to take place in Normandy sometime in 1944. The whole strategy was shot through with compromise, but easily the most controversial element was the combined bomber offensive, Operation POINTBLANK, which set forth a plan for the round-the-clock bombing of Germany, combining precision daylight attacks by the U.S. Eighth Air Force with a night area bombing campaign conducted by RAF Bomber Command. Few outside the U.S. Army Air Forces had much confidence in their ability to mount a successful daylight strategic bombing campaign.

One thing about which the Allied planners could be certain, though: the Germans knew they were coming. There was little doubt in the minds of Adolf Hitler and the German High Command that the conquest of North Africa (completed early in 1943) would be followed by a buildup for an all-out assault on Western Europe. The only questions were where and when.

Moving to counter the German offensive into the Ardennes, the US 289th Infantry Division advances through a Belgian forest in December 1944.

Whereas British bombers struck at German targets under cover of night, the U.S. Army Air Forces mounted daylight raids, relying on the massed firepower of its bomber formations to get through to the target and return. Bomber gunners such as this one were often confronted with German fighter attacks all the way to the target and all the way back again. Until adequate fighter escorts could be provided, casualties were heavy. The Allied dorsal turret gunner shown here would have scant opportunity to use his camera once the German fighter attacks began.

Under such circumstances, Allied intelligence was to play a critical role. For the Allied assault on German-occupied Europe to have any hope of success, invasion planners had to have detailed knowledge about the scale, scope, and location of the German defenses. The timing and location of the invasion had to be kept secret and, if possible, the enemy had to be persuaded to concentrate his defenses elsewhere. Agents and saboteurs had to be organized and positioned to help the troops once they came ashore. But the most immediate task was to support the strategic bombing offensive.

## The Economic Objectives Unit and the Bombing of Germany

The U.S. Army Air Forces had long advocated a strategy of daylight bombing against the enemy's war industry. Central to this plan was the assumption that it was possible to identify discrete "bottlenecks" in the German war industry, the destruction of which would bring down the whole of the enemy's war economy like a house of cards. This U.S. approach of narrowly focused attacks on well-defined sectors of German industry was in direct contradiction to the British strategy of wide-ranging night attacks on every sector of German industry. Together, the two bombing campaigns made a deadly combination that, by the end of the war, left German cities little more than barely habitable mounds of rubble.

But for air force planners, the question was how to find the bottlenecks. For a sophisticated, heavily industrialized war economy like Germany's, there were as many answers to that question as there were potential targets. The Royal Air Force largely dismissed the whole idea of nuanced target selection in favor of night area attacks on German cities. The British Ministry of Economic Warfare (MEW), following its "one-man brain trust," anthropologist Sir Solly Zuckerman, advocated attacks on German railroad-marshalling yards. The U.S. planners opted for attacks on the German ball-bearing industry. Virtually everything the Germans built used ball bearings, so if production of this vital commodity could be halted, German war production as a

whole would come screeching to a halt. Eighth Air Force attacks on the ball-bearing works at Schweinfurt in August and September 1943 came close to doing just that, but the unescorted bombers suffered losses so appalling that the offensive was aborted before it could be brought to fruition.

Over the winter of 1943 to 1944, the Eighth Air Force rebounded and, in February 1944, decisively defeated the German fighter force. As longer days and spring weather approached, the question again became how best to attack German industry.

Into the breach stepped the Economic Objectives Unit (EOU), a top-secret OSS detachment operating behind closed doors in the U.S. London embassy. The EOU had been formed in 1942 as an intelligence unit to develop systematic target selection criteria for the U.S. Strategic Air Forces in Europe. Typical of OSS research units, EOU was made up of arrogant, unruly,

LEFT: The B-17 Flying Fortress was designed for high-altitude, precision bombing attacks against defended targets. For the attacks to be successful, however, the targets first had to be identified and located. BELOW LEFT: After an attack, the damage had to be assessed and the decision made whether and when to strike the target again. The intelligence analysts who performed these often mundane tasks seldom participated in the attacks they helped to plan, but were nonetheless just as important to the success of the Allied bombing offensive as the men who flew the planes.

# Operation MINCEMEAT

On April 30, 1943, the body of a Royal Marine officer, "Major Martin" washed up on the coast of Spain, near Huelva. Although Spain was a declared nonbelligerent in the war, the German consul was immediately notified. The corpse was delivered to the British consul in the area shortly after its discovery, but the officer's briefcase was not returned for some weeks, during which time the Spanish and German intelligence services thoroughly examined its contents. In the briefcase were papers discussing the planned Allied invasion of Sardinia. Having obtained these documents, the Abwehr immediately passed them to the intelligence division of the German General Staff, where the *Kurierfund* ("Courier Find") was received with great interest.

Actually, the operation was a hoax, arranged by the XX-committee and carried out by Lieutenant Commander Ewen Montagu. The body was that of a British officer who had been killed in an air crash and then recovered by the British. Suitably outfitted in the uniform of a Royal Marine major, the corpse was given a briefcase full of papers and other random identifying pieces of "pocket litter" designed to give credence to his fictional identity. "Major Martin" had been dropped off the Spanish coast by a British submarine. All the papers were false, and were placed there to convey exactly the impression that they did; the Germans and, indeed, the Spanish, had reacted in precisely the way it had been hoped they would. The XX-committee was elated when ULTRA confirmed the following month that the German General Staff had swallowed the false information whole.

In truth, MINCEMEAT probably did little to alter German dispositions. The Germans did take MINCEMEAT as credible evidence that the landings they anticipated on Italian soil would take place in Sardinia. But by the time Allied forces landed in Sicily the following July, German forces were stretched pretty thin, and Hitler, in particular, had lost whatever faith he had once had in his Italian ally. Although there were only two divisions present in Sicily (both badly beaten up in North Africa), there is little evidence that the Germans would have committed more to the defense of the island had they been convinced it would be the next Allied target. However, MINCEMEAT did help to persuade the Germans that there was a broader Allied commitment to the Mediterranean than was in fact the case. German garrisons in the Balkans were probably larger than they would have been otherwise, diverting troops from the actual invasion sites in Normandy.

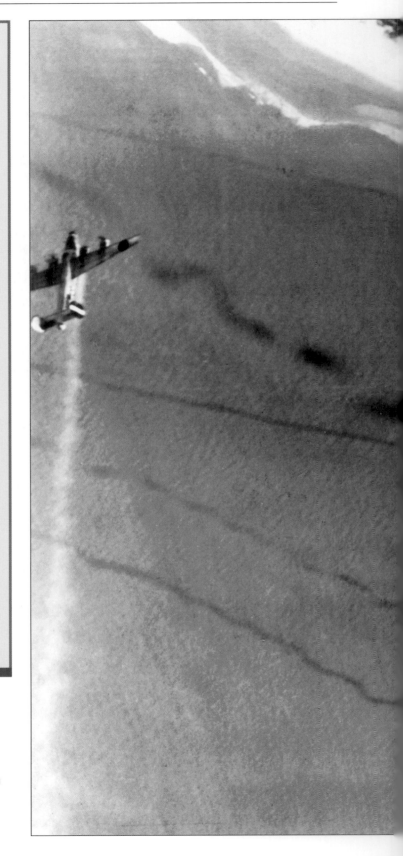

U.S. B-24 Liberator heavy bombers attack French coastal targets. In the summer of 1944, American planners were torn between using the heavy bomber force to attack French coastal defenses and striking more "strategic" targets, such as the German oil industry. Although weakened, German air defenses remained effective right up until the end of the war and losses had to be expected at all times.

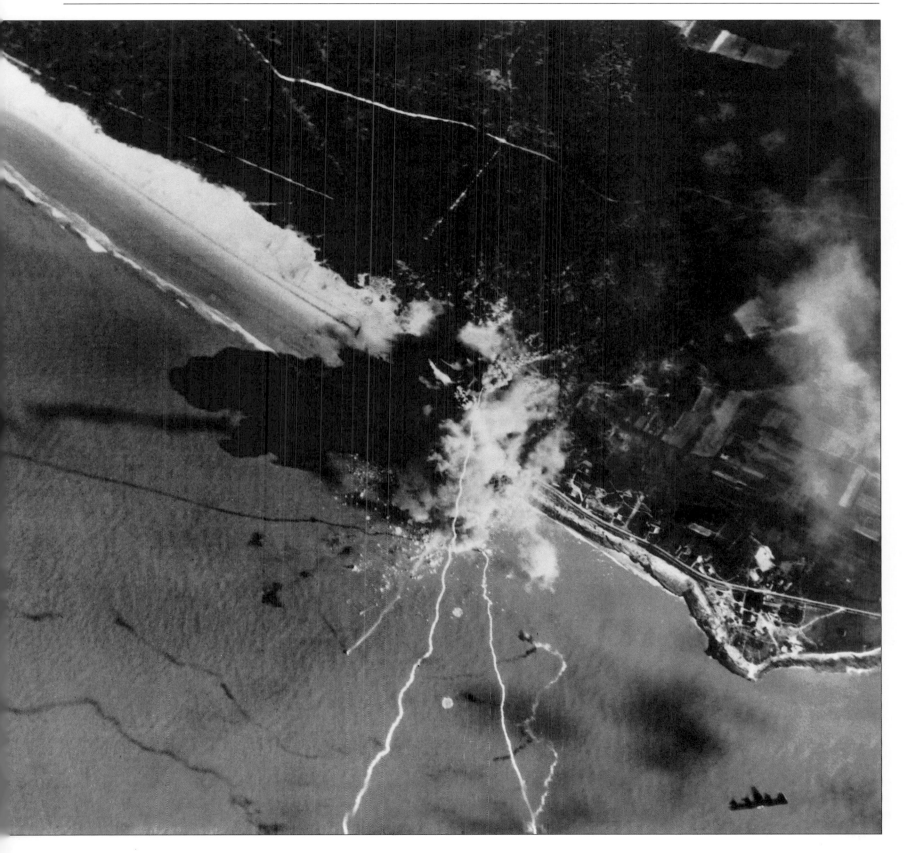

## Eric Siegfried Erickson

An American-born oil businessman of Swedish extraction, Eric Erickson was one of the most effective agents available to the OSS in World War II. "Red" Erickson (the nickname referred to both his quick temper and the Viking "Eric the Red") was born in Brooklyn, New York, but moved to Sweden after World War I, where he was named managing director of Texaco's operations. He eventually started an oil-importing company and in 1936 became a Swedish citizen. In 1939 he was recruited as an agent by U.S. military intelligence, to report on German economic activity in Sweden and on the oil industry in particular.

Over the next two years, Erickson cultivated relationships with numerous high-ranking Nazis, including such grim luminaries as Heinrich Himmler. Between 1941 and 1944, he made more than thirty trips into Germany and German-occupied Europe, all the while collecting information on the German war industry to pass to his OSS handlers in Stockholm. In 1944 he concocted a plan to build a German oil refinery in Sweden, where it would be safe from the Allied bombers that were then ravaging the German oil industry. The idea was a brilliant scheme that seemingly combined profit and Swedish national interest (Sweden was short of oil and other commodities because of the Allied blockade) with the needs of the German war economy. Of course, Erickson had no intention of actually building the refinery (at that stage of the war, the idea was no more than a pipe dream anyway), but the required negotiations kept him flying between Stockholm and Berlin for months and brought him more contacts inside German industry. During these trips, Erickson made detailed presentations about the proposed refinery, all with charts, maps, and graphs produced by OSS Stockholm.

Erickson's pose as a Nazi collaborator and war profiteer cost him most of his friends in Sweden, but at war's end his role was revealed. For a time, he became something of a celebrity: in 1958, journalist Alexander Klein published *The Counterfeit Traitor*, a semifictional account of Erickson's exploits, which was made into a popular film in 1962.

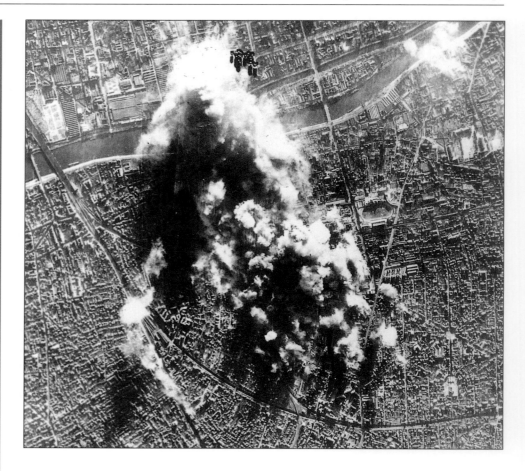

Timely intelligence was vital to the conduct of the strategic air offensive against German-occupied Europe. Here, bombers strike the Hispano-Suiza engine plant in Paris. The U.S. technique of precision bombing made it possible to attack single targets rather than whole cities (as the British Royal Air Force did), but it also made it necessary to identify and locate the targets precisely.

and brilliant academics (economists mainly), whose numbers included Walt W. Rostow and Charles P. Kindleberger.

At EOU's head was Army Air Forces Colonel Richard D'Oyly Hughes, a naturalized Englishman. His brother, Royal Navy Captain Guy D'Oyly Hughes, had been killed when his ship, the aircraft carrier *Glorious*, was sunk by the battleships *Scharnhorst* and *Gneisenau* off the coast of Norway. As a result, Richard Hughes had little sympathy for Germans and was quite prepared to see their cities pounded into dust. His accent and rumpled U.S. Army uniform, bedecked with British decorations, caused considerable confusion in London, but his transatlantic connections made him an effective player in the strategic debates that raged in the Allied High Command.

Assembling the Economic Objectives Unit in 1942, Hughes put the unit to work preparing "aiming point reports" that amounted simply to a systematic analysis of the whole of the German war economy. It was yet another wartime irony that the EOU, like most of the OSS, was denied access to crucial ULTRA information. Instead, EOU analysts relied primarily on reconnaissance photos, agent reports, and what they could glean from British experience. In the end, the EOU concluded that the best way to defeat Germany was to take out its oil supplies, so they put together what was known as the "oil plan." But Lieutenant General Ira Eaker, the Eighth Air Force commander, opted to take his own staff's advice and sent his bombers on the ill-fated missions to attack ball-bearing plants in Germany.

Eaker was promoted following the defeats over Schweinfurt, and replaced by Lieutenant General Carl

Spaatz. Spaatz accepted the oil plan, but was forced to hold off until the summer of 1944 by the need to support the landings in Normandy. That summer, Eighth Air Force bombers were finally unleashed against the German oil refineries. The results were dramatic: monthly German oil production went from 180,000 tons (163.4 million kg) in March 1944 to 10,000 tons (9.1 million kg) in September. The Economic Objectives Unit was proved correct: at war's end, Allied troops walked the streets and airfields of Germany and wondered at the row upon row of newly completed aircraft, tanks, and vehicles of every description, all immobilized and abandoned for lack of fuel.

Sometimes, even the best intelligence is of no use. On September 6, 1943, Eighth Air Force B-17s and B-24s struck German industrial targets in and around Stuttgart. Clouds obscured the targets and broke up the formations, a situation that was exploited to the fullest by the defending German fighters. Of 322 heavy bombers dispatched on the mission, 45 were shot down and 116 were damaged—some beyond repair. 333 American airmen were shot down over enemy territory and killed or taken prisoner. Losses such as these were unendurable and produced the "Fall Crisis" in Eighth Air Force Bomber Command.

# Operation FORTITUDE

ULTRA proved a priceless asset in the preparations for the invasion of Europe. Although the Germans naturally preferred to use land lines whenever possible, enough ULTRA intercepts were collected over 1943 and 1944 to identify all but two of the divisions in France, and especially those manning the coastal defenses. ULTRA also proved invaluable in Operation FORTITUDE, the plan for deceiving the German High Command about the Allies' ultimate intentions for the invasion of Europe. The purpose of FORTITUDE was to mask the landings in Normandy by convincing the Germans that the actual invasion would occur in the Pas de Calais, and to keep the enemy in doubt about the actual timing of the assault. After D-Day, it was hoped that the cumulative effect of FORTITUDE would be so great that the Germans would see the Normandy landings as a feint, launched as a precursor to the real assault.

The principal means used to implement FORTITUDE came in the form of the double agents of the XX-committee. Over 1943 and 1944, their reporting built up a seemingly complete, and utterly false, picture of Allied strengths and the plans for the invasion of Europe. ULTRA provided a means of checking the success of this campaign of deception, revealing German reactions to the information received. Knowing this, Allied intelligence officers could better craft their operations to fit German preconceptions. Without ULTRA, it is doubtful that FORTITUDE would have succeeded to the extent that it did.

At the heart of FORTITUDE was the London Controlling Section (LCS), perhaps the smallest of the secret organizations set up by the British to assist in the war against Germany. The LCS created the false stories put out to the Germans (mainly through the double agents controlled by the XX-committee). The LCS also had to keep track of the stories that were put out, to make sure they were consistent and did not undermine some other war operations (real or fanciful). There were two principal deception plans: FORTITUDE NORTH, which was a preliminary to the actual invasion, and FORTITUDE SOUTH, which created the fiction of imminent landings in the Pas de Calais.

FORTITUDE NORTH called for a fictional invasion of Norway. The idea was to draw troops into Norway

# Agent Operations

As the Anglo-American armies were built up for the great invasion of Western Europe, the British and American intelligence services organized to support active military operations. Although both the American OSS and the British SOE had actively supported the resistance movements on the ground as best they could throughout the war, the tight control exercised under the Axis occupation—especially in German-held areas—had greatly limited the scope of their activities, except in remote areas where weather or terrain hindered the occupying troops. But in the fluid situation following the seaborne invasion, it was anticipated that much more could be achieved. Thus, when the troops hit the beach on June 6, 1944, specially trained teams of agents were waiting for them in France: uniformed "Jedburgh" teams of three agents (one American, one British, and usually one French) parachuted in before the invasion to conduct acts of sabotage and disrupt enemy communications behind the lines. For the most part, these agents kept a very low profile until the invasion actually occurred; then they moved into action, helping to isolate the beachhead from enemy reinforcements and supplies and to spread confusion in the enemy's rear area.

Also on the ground in France awaiting the arrival of Allied troops were two-man "Sussex" teams, made up of Free French agents recruited mainly in North Africa. Wearing civilian clothes, these teams moved

Advancing American troops pick up a Free French agent and return him to headquarters for debriefing—and a well-earned rest.

freely throughout their native French countryside, collecting tactical intelligence that they reported by wireless to Allied military intelligence units moving ashore with the advancing armies. Most were overrun by mid-July, so a second wave, dubbed "Proust" teams, was dropped in with the same mission as the first, but operating more deeply inside enemy-occupied France.

In the winter of 1944, the successful advance of the Allied armies made it possible (and even necessary) to contemplate the penetration of Nazi Germany itself, hitherto a nearly impossible task. The head of the OSS, William Donovan, had a unit in place intended to do just that. This was the only wholly OSS-agent operation in Western Europe—all others had been mounted in cooperation with the British SOE. It was also to be the most dangerous: unlike in occupied France, agents on the ground in Nazi Germany could expect little but hostility from the local populace. Germans who had lost loved ones in the war, or who had sons, brothers, or husbands still at the front, did not have to be loyal supporters of Hitler to bitterly hate any spies and possible saboteurs they might find in their midst. Agents in Germany would have to be virtually undetectable to survive.

For control of this operation, Donovan had in mind a brash, young navy lieutenant who had been rattling around his office since the start of the war, William J. Casey (who was later named director of the Central Intelligence Agency under Ronald Reagan). Casey set about recruiting agents from the vast pool of exiles from Hitler's Europe: the wide-scale use of conscripted labor in Germany made *Fremdearbeiter* ("foreign worker") an ideal cover.

To his dismay, the deeply conservative Casey discovered that his best potential agents were communists. This did not bother the pragmatic Donovan one whit: he knew that the communists would get the job done. So Casey swallowed his ideological misgivings and set about infiltrating the Reich. By April 1945, he had more than 100 agent teams working inside German territory. Casualties were remarkably light (less than 5 percent), but the results were disappointing: the intelligence collected tended to be tactical in nature, or sometimes political. The agents could report on bomb damage, on the covert movement of German troops, and on the whereabouts of local Nazi leaders—the latter information being of increasing importance as the war wound down and the victorious Allied powers began preparing for the postwar trials to be held at Nüremberg. Casey himself acknowledged that his operations had done little to shorten the war, but they did probably save some lives, an outcome of no small value.

before the actual invasion took place in France. Because of the distances involved, the poor transportation systems available, and the danger to the Germans involved in moving large bodies of troops by sea, any forces deployed to Norway would tend to stay there and probably would not be available for other theaters.

To make the attack on Norway, a fictional Fourth Army was created, under Lieutenant General Sir Andrew Thorne, based in Edinburgh. Composed of eight equally notional divisions, the Fourth Army was to land in Narvik and Stavanger, liberate Norway, and open the way for an advance south into Denmark. Because the Scottish weather prevented reliable air reconnaissance, little effort was made to prepare any visual deceptions, but the existence of the Fourth Army was fully recorded using double-agent reporting and false radio transmissions.

FORTITUDE SOUTH was more directly related to the landings in Normandy, supporting, as it did, the idea of a landing in the Pas de Calais. A complete First U.S. Army Group (FUSAG) was created under the command of the American army's premier tank officer, Lieutenant General George S. Patton Jr. FUSAG was composed of two real armies, the First Canadian Army (actually part of British General Montgomery's Twenty-first Army Group) and the Third U.S. Army, being formed to follow up and exploit the beachhead won by the invading forces into France. Patton would later command the Third Army in battle. Both armies were considerably augmented by dummy airfields and military bases replete with bogus equipment and, of course, the full panoply of radio traffic appropriate to a military organization of its supposed size and magnitude. All this was considered necessary to fool German signals intelligence organizations and Luftwaffe reconnaissance, which was still operating at that stage of the war.

FORTITUDE NORTH benefited from Hitler's intuitive belief that the first Allied landing would be in Norway. But if the scheme gave substance to that belief, it did not succeed in persuading the Germans to reinforce their garrison there beyond what they had already considered necessary. FORTITUDE SOUTH, by contrast, succeeded brilliantly in its task. When the Allied landings took place in Normandy, not one German soldier was moved

General George S. Patton Jr. eventually commanded the U.S. Third Army in France. Before the Normandy Invasion, however, he was in command of the nonexistent First US Army Group (FUSAG), assembled for the ostensible purpose of making landings in the Pas de Calais. Here, Patton plays with his bull terrier, the cowardly William the Conqueror ("Willie").

from the Pas de Calais area to reinforce the Normandy defenses. Even more important, so convinced of the Pas de Calais landing was the German commander in France, Field Marshal Gerd von Rundstedt, that he held three Panzer Divisions back from Normandy for two weeks, awaiting the anticipated landings in Pas de Calais. By the time the Germans realized that the Normandy landings constituted the actual invasion, the bridgehead had been established and the invasion was a success.

Other deception plans propagated by London Control Station included MINCEMEAT, which masked the invasion of Sicily in 1943, and ZEPPELIN, put forward as a Mediterranean alternative to OVERLORD, the invasion in Normandy.

Convinced by Allied deception efforts that the real invasion would come elsewhere, the German high command with-held reinforcements from Normandy at a critical moment in the campaign. Dummy tanks such as these helped to deceive German intelligence.

# ULTRA and the Campaign in France and Germany

As the Allied armies moved across France and up to the Rhine, ULTRA remained the best source of intelligence at every level from tactical to strategic. The disruption of German land communications due to bombing (and, of course, the Jedburgh teams) meant that the Germans were driven to rely heavily on wireless for every form of tactical and operational message. This was exactly the kind of situation for which the ENIGMA machine had been devised, and the Nazis used it in the belief that their signals could not be read. For Allied intelligence, the biggest problem became processing and dissemi-nating the information obtained by the cryptanalysts. Intelligence officers could not keep up with the con-stantly shifting air and tank battles taking place in Normandy. This had direct effects on the battlefront. In one controversial decision, an American commander, Omar Bradley, ordered a halt to Patton's advancing Third Army just as it was about to meet up with Montgomery's troops and trap the German Seventh Army in the Falaise pocket. Bradley feared that the American troops coming up from the south might find themselves in combat with their Canadian allies coming down from the north. The result was that the German Seventh Army escaped the trap being set for it and regrouped to fight on deeper in France. By the end of September, however, France had mostly been liberated and the Allied armies were girding themselves to cross the Rhine.

Some of the very real difficulties in interpreting intelligence in the midst of fluid military operations were further seen beginning in October 1944, as ULTRA began to provide evidence of a buildup in northern Germany, across the Rhine from Belgium. In retrospect, it is clear that ULTRA was showing the coordinated train and road movements of the last German offensive of the war, Operation Wacht am Rhein. But German security was tight and the available information seemed far from unambiguous at the time. The Germans also were aided in their attempt at secrecy by the sheer folly of the plan: Allied commanders were agreed that German resources were so depleted that the Germans would have been far

better off remaining on the defensive. At Allied headquarters, it was widely believed that the buildup was in
preparation for a counterattack in the face of the next
Allied offensive.

The German Ardennes offensive on December 16,
1944, thus came as a surprise, despite the intelligence
warnings that had preceded it. The Ardennes had been
left lightly garrisoned, as a calculated risk, to allow the
British and American forces to pursue their objectives
to the north and south. The German attack simply
created a pocket from which there was no escape.
German troops advanced as long as the weather prevented air support from being called in, but were
unable to overcome the resistance of the U.S. 101st
Airborne Division in Bastogne and slowed as soon as
they ran into the Allied forces adjacent to the "bulge"
they had created. Hitler's insistence on continuing the
attack long after it had obviously failed dissipated
Germany's last remaining reserves. Although months
of hard fighting remained, by the end of the year, the
war in Western Europe was all but over. Meanwhile,
the relentless advance of the Soviet armies from the
East guaranteed the defeat of Hitler's Reich. On April
25, 1945, Berlin was surrounded by Soviet troops.
On April 30, Hitler committed suicide, and by May 8
Germany had surrendered.

OPPOSITE: As German resistance in France collapsed, irregular forces came into
their own. Perhaps the French resistance's finest hour was the role they played in
the liberation of Paris. As the Germans prepared to evacuate the capital, French
fighters—mainly Communists—inside the city rose up to harass and delay their
retreat, while special liaison teams met with the Allied columns advancing on the
city to guide them in. The rapid, decisive French action may have prevented the
Germans from carrying out the planned demolition of the city. Here a French resistance fighter guides an American combat team into the city.
ABOVE RIGHT: Massed for one last offensive during the Battle of the Bulge
(Operation Wacht am Rhein), SS troops advance on Malmedy in the Ardennes.
The German attack surprised Western intelligence analysts, but dissipated
Germany's last reserves. BELOW RIGHT: German prisoners of war after defeat in
the 1944 Ardennes offensive. In the long run, this hopeless German attempt to
regain the initiative in the West only hastened defeat on both the Western and
Eastern fronts.

# Chapter 8

# ULTRA and the Invasion of Japan

ON THE PACIFIC FRONT, THE OUTCOME OF THE BATTLE OF MIDWAY FORESHADOWED
the decisive defeat of Japan in the Pacific War. Although the Imperial Japanese Navy fought tenaciously over 1942 and 1943 in the Solomons and elsewhere, inflicting individual defeats on
the U.S. Navy, at Midway Japan forever lost its chance to win the war. From that point on, the
Western Allies, and especially the United States, grew steadily stronger, while the strength of
the Japanese empire slowly eroded away. The war in China became a backwater. The strength
of the Japanese forces there was slowly drawn down to feed the Pacific War until, by the time
the Soviet Union declared war against Japan in August 1945, there was nothing left of Japan's
military might but a hollow shell.

Throughout 1944, the Japanese leadership fought on with increasing despair, as the Allied
offensive drove steadily across the Pacific, into the Philippines, and
eventually drew near to Japan itself. In the Philippines, the Japanese air
forces launched the first of their *kamikaze*, or suicide, attacks, against
the American fleet, increasingly the only means they had of penetrating
the American defensive screens. In April 1945, Anglo-American naval
forces launched an assault on Okinawa, an island closely identified with
the Japanese home islands themselves. That month, too, the battleship
*Yamato*, the last effective heavy unit in the Japanese navy, expended
herself in a suicide mission against the American fleet.

American soldiers pick their
way through a pile of Japanese
wreckage. On top of the pile
is the remains of a G3M2 Nell
bomber, the same kind of
plane that was used to sink
the *Prince of Wales* and the
*Repulse* in 1941.

By the end of World War II, aircraft carriers had replaced battleships as the measure of modern sea power. Superior U.S. industrial capacity meant that the Americans were able to deploy more and better carriers than the Japanese, and had the wherewithal to take them across the Pacific to Japan. After 1943—at the latest—the Allies did not need their superior intelligence capability to defeat Japan, but more and more were concerned with saving as many lives as possible. Japanese kamikaze, or suicide, attacks, such as the one that damaged this aircraft carrier (left), only reinforced this determination.

The following month, Japanese representatives in Switzerland approached the head of the OSS mission in Bern, Allen Dulles. in an attempt to secure a negotiated peace, using the good offices of Per Jacobsson, the Swedish representative on the board of the Bank of International Settlements. The Japanese approached Dulles because he had helped to broker the surrender of the German forces in northern Italy. Dulles was, however, constrained by the Allied demands for unconditional Japanese surrender. At about the same time, MAGIC intercepts revealed efforts to persuade Moscow to negotiate a peace, but Stalin had pledged to enter the Pacific War himself—and he did so. All the same, the Japanese tried desperately over the summer of 1945 to broker a peace, stopping just short of unconditional surrender. Time and again, the sticking point was the preservation of the Imperial system and guarantees for the protection of the emperor's person, without which fanatical elements in Tokyo would never agree to a surrender.

Meanwhile, the U.S. chief of naval operations, Fleet Admiral Ernest J. King, and the army chief of staff, General of the Army George C. Marshall, were debating how best to defeat Japan. King felt that a combined air-naval blockade would suffice, while Marshall argued for invasion. Over April 1945, in response to a planning directive issued by President Roosevelt, the naval and military staffs drew up a plan for a two-stage invasion of the home islands. Operation Olympic, an invasion of the southernmost island, Kyushu, was to begin no later than November 1, 1945 (any further delay would mean postponement until the following year, because of the weather). Olympic was to be followed on March 1, 1946, by Coronet, the invasion of the main Japanese home island of Honshu. Casualty estimates were high: 133,000 dead and wounded for Olympic, 88,000 for Coronet. Although the Japanese army was effectively beaten, Japanese troops were expected to resist with the tenacity they had displayed in battles all across the Pacific.

As before, signals intelligence was the only means of evaluating what was going on in Japan. Although Anglo-American cryptanalysts never read the Japanese

Although Western intelligence analysts had been stunned by the dimensions of the giant Japanese battleship *Yamato*, the ship was actually irrelevant to the conduct of the war in the Pacific.

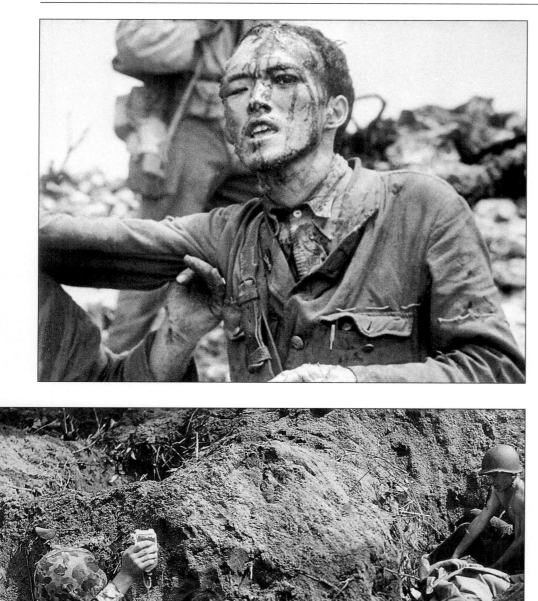

naval codes with the same ease that they penetrated those of the European Axis, after 1942 they were read with reasonable regularity. Japanese army codes were not broken until April 1943, after which they were readable for the rest of the war.

The signals intelligence thus obtained showed the obvious—that the Japanese were expecting an invasion. An April message from the German naval attaché in Tokyo (and hence in a German ENIGMA cipher) described Japanese expectations: invasion of Okinawa followed by a landing on Honshu. By mid-April, it was obvious that the Japanese now expected the initial assault to be on Kyushu: reports showed troops being moved there from Manchuria. By mid-May signals intelligence estimates gave a total of some 246,000 combat troops on Kyushu, to be augmented by an additional 100,000 by November 1. Meanwhile, other intercepts showed that the Japanese were mining coastal waters off the likely invasion sites. Still others showed that 2,000 kamikaze aircraft were being assembled for a last-ditch defense of the homeland, while bases were being built for *Kaiten*—suicide torpedoes.

Although President Harry S Truman (who took office after Roosevelt's death on April 12, 1945) approved the plans for Olympic on June 18, 1945, further reports over the summer showed that the invasion was going to be a tough proposition. By August 2, some 545,000 combat troops were identified on Kyushu, with perhaps another 40,000 in unlocated units. But none of this material showed the composition of these units, reported how well they were armed, or gave a good idea of how well they would fight. Given the prior experience of the Pacific War, however, it was hard not to expect the worst.

Even as these plans were being prepared, American B-29 long-range strategic bombers were roaming at will over Japanese cities, now virtually devoid of fighter protection. The most destructive raids occurred over the nights of March 9 and 10, when B-29s dropped more than 2,000 tons (1.8 million kg) of incendiary bombs, burning out 15.8 square miles (40.9 square km) of Tokyo and killing nearly 84,000 people, with another 41,000 injured. More than 1 million people were left homeless. Raids continued at this level over the spring and summer, until the first atomic bomb was dropped

OPPOSITE TOP: The ferocity of Japanese resistance on Okinawa and Iwo Jima convinced Western planners that invasion of the Japanese homeland would be extremely costly. Here, a Japanese Lieutenant surrenders only after being badly wounded. OPPOSITE BOTTOM: American wounded receive treatment under primitive conditions on Bougainville. LEFT: To avoid further heavy casualties, U.S. planners were prepared to devastate Japan from the air. This photograph shows Tokyo flattened after the fire-bombing raids of March 9-10, 1945. In many respects, the damage done in this raid was worse than that done by the atomic bombs used on Hiroshima and Nagasaki.

on Hiroshima on August 6. In this raid, 4.7 square miles (12.2 square km) in the center of the city were destroyed and 72,000 people were killed, with another 68,000 injured. The atomic devastation continued at Nagasaki three days later, where 1.45 square miles (3.8 square km) of the city were destroyed and 35,000 people were killed and 66,000 injured. Five days later, their cities in ruins, the Japanese government sued for peace and agreed to an unconditional surrender.

The American military was spared the agony of finding out whether the casualty figures they had prepared for the invasion of Japan were correct.

## Suggestions for Further Reading

More than fifty years after the end of the war, the history of World War II intelligence remains a subject that has not yet been fully explored. A few of the most significant and useful works in the field are:

Ralph F. Bennett. *Ultra and Mediterranean Strategy*. New York: Morrow, 1989.

Ralph F. Bennett. *Ultra in the West: The Normandy Campaign of 1944–45*. New York: Scribner's, 1980.

Carl Boyd. *Hitler's Japanese Confidant: General Oshima Hiroshi and Magic Intelligence, 1941–1945*. Lawrence, KS: University Press of Kansas, 1993.

F.H. Hinsley, et.al. *British Intelligence in the Second World War, 5 Vols*. London: HMSO, 1979–90.

Capt. W.J. Holmes. *Double-edged Secrets: U.S. Naval Intelligence Operations in the Pacific During World War II*. Annapolis, MD: Naval Institute Press, 1979.

David Kahn. *Hitler's Spies: German Military Intelligence in World War II*. New York: Macmillan, 1978.

David Kahn, *Seizing the Enigma: The Race to Break the German U-Boat Codes, 1939–1943*. Boston: Houghton Mifflin, 1991.

Wladyslaw Kozaczuk. *Enigma: How the German Cipher was Broken and How It Was Read by the Allies in World War II*. Frederick, MD: University Publications of America, 1984.

Ronald Lewin. *The American Magic: Codes, Ciphers and the Defeat of Japan*. New York: Farrar, Straus and Giroux, 1982.

Douglas J. MacEachin. *The Final Months of War with Japan: Signals Intelligence, U.S. Invasion Planning, and the A-Bomb Decision*. Washington, D.C.: Center for the Study of Intelligence, 1998.

Janusz Piekalkiewicz. *Rommel and the Secret War in North Africa, 1941–1943: Secret Intelligence in the North African Campaign*. West Chester, PA: Schiffer Military History, 1992.

John Winton. *Ultra at Sea: How Breaking the Nazi Code Affected Allied Naval Strategy During World War II*. New York: William Morrow, 1988.

## Photo Credits

## Illustration Credits

# Index